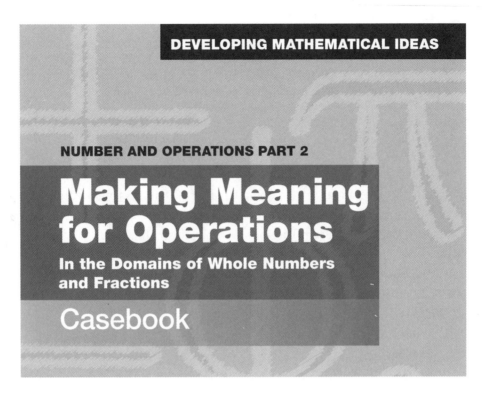

DEVELOPING MATHEMATICAL IDEAS

NUMBER AND OPERATIONS PART 2

Making Meaning for Operations

In the Domains of Whole Numbers and Fractions

Casebook

A collaborative project by the staff and
participants of Teaching to the Big Ideas

Principal Investigators
Deborah Schifter
Virginia Bastable
Susan Jo Russell

**NATIONAL COUNCIL OF
TEACHERS OF MATHEMATICS**

Copyright © 2016 by
The Education Development Center, Inc.
Published by
The National Council of Teachers of Mathematics, Inc.
1906 Association Drive, Reston, VA 20191-1502
(703) 620-9840; (800) 235-7566; www.nctm.org
Previous editions published by Pearson Education, Inc.

Library of Congress Cataloging-in-Publication Data

Names: Schifter, Deborah. | Bastable, Virginia. | Russell, Susan Jo.

Title: Making meaning for operations : in the domains of whole numbers and fractions casebook :
updated 2016 : a collaborative project / by the staff and participants of Teaching to the Big Ideas ;
principal investigators, Deborah Schifter, Virginia Bastable, Susan Jo Russell.

Description: Reston, VA : The National Council of Teachers of Mathematics, [2016] | Series: Developing mathematical ideas. Number and operations ; part 2

Identifiers: LCCN 2016019368 (print) | LCCN 2016023708 (ebook) | ISBN 9780873539340 (pbk.) |
ISBN 9780873539555 ()

Subjects: LCSH: Arithmetic--Study and teaching (Elementary) | Addition. | Subtraction. | Multiplication. | Division. | Fractions.

Classification: LCC QA115 .S328 2016 (print) | LCC QA115 (ebook) | DDC 372.7--dc23

LC record available at https://lccn.loc.gov/2016019368

The National Council of Teachers of Mathematics is the public voice of mathematics education,
supporting teachers to ensure equitable mathematics learning of the highest quality for all students
through vision, leadership, professional development, and research.

Printed in the United States of America

Teaching to the Big Ideas

TEACHER COLLABORATORS   Allan Arnaboldi, Audrey Barzey, Nancy Buell, Rose Christiansen, Lisette Colon, Francis Cooper, Marcia Estelle, Victoria Fink, Christopher Fraley, Marta Garcia, Gail Gilmore, Scott Hendrickson, Nancy Horowitz, Kirsten Lee Howard, Bruce Kamerer, Robin Musser, Anne Marie O'Reilly, Mark Paige, Angela Philactos, Margaret Riddle, Nicole Rigelman, Jan Rook, Sherry Sadjak, Karen Schweitzer, Malia Scott, Lisa Seyferth, Elizabeth Sweeney, Polly Wagner, Carol Walker, Steve Walkowicz, Dee Watson representing the public schools of Amherst (Mass.), Belchertown (Mass.), Bismarck (N.Dak.), Boston (Mass.), Brookline (Mass.), Buncomb County (N.C.), Newton (Mass.), Northampton (Mass.), Southampton (Mass.), Springfield (Mass.), Westfield (Mass.), Williamsburg (Mass.) and the Atrium School (Mass.), Brigham Young University (Utah), and Portland State University (Ore.)

REVIEWERS AND CONSULTANTS   Tami Bird (Jordan Public Schools, Utah), Thomas Carpenter (University of Wisconsin), Susan Empson (University of Texas), Michael Flynn (Mount Holyoke College, Mass.), Benjamin Ford (Sonoma State University, Calif.), Connie Henry (Boston Public Schools), Sterling Hilton (Brigham Young University, Utah), Laurie King (Greece Central Public Schools, N.Y.), Barbara Kuehl (Salt Lake City Public Schools), Anita Lenges (University of Washington), (Jill Bodner Lester (Mount Holyoke College, Mass.), James Lewis (University of Nebraska), Amy Morse (Education Development Center, Mass.), Katie Rafferty (Houston Independent School District, Tex.), Ann Ruggiero (Boston Public Schools), Sherry Sajdak (Boston Public Schools), Susan Bush Smith (Mount Holyoke College, Mass.), Vicki Smith (Salt Lake City Public Schools), Virginia Stimpson (University of Washington), Joy Whitenack (Virginia Commonwealth University), Lisa Yaffee (independent consultant, Vt.)

PROJECT EDITOR, NCTM • Maryanne Bannon
PROJECT EDITOR, Dale Seymour Publications/Pearson Learning Group • Beverly Cory
VIDEO DEVELOPMENT • David Smith (David Smith Productions)

 **National Science Foundation**

This work was supported by the National Science Foundation under Grant Nos. ESI-9254393 (awarded to EDC), ESI-0095450 (awarded to TERC), and ESI-0242609 (awarded to EDC). Any opinions, findings, conclusions, or recommendations expressed here are those of the authors and do not necessarily reflect the views of the National Science Foundation.

Additional support was provided by the ExxonMobil Foundation and the Bill and Melinda Gates Foundation.

Contents

Contents

Introduction

The cases in *Making Meaning for Operations* concentrate on such questions as "What kinds of actions and situations are modeled by addition, subtraction, multiplication, and division?" and "How do students, as they work with such situations, come to understand the operations?" One seminar facilitator put it this way: "*Making Meaning for Operations* challenges our definition of operation. It brings operation out of a computation framework into a 'meaning' framework."

The casebook begins with a look at young children's counting strategies as they address problems that they will later solve by adding and subtracting. Chapters 1 and 2 examine the different types of situations that are modeled by whole number addition/subtraction and multiplication/division. But as illustrated by the cases in chapter 3, the operation of division introduces a new kind of number, fractions, when the division doesn't come out evenly. Chapter 4 concentrates on how the numerator and denominator of a fraction together determine the size of the fraction.

The latter part of the casebook, chapters 5 through 7, revisits the operations in the context of fractions. What whole number ideas, issues, and generalizations need to be refined or revised once the work is extended to include fractions? For example, how do you now make sense of multiplying when the numbers being multiplied create a product smaller than the numbers you started with?

The cases were all written by elementary and middle school teachers, describing events from their own classrooms. The teacher-authors were inquiring into how their own students come to make meaning for operations. Writing these cases was part of that process of inquiry, and the teachers came together on a regular basis to read and discuss one another's work.

The casebook concludes with a chapter called "Highlights of Related Research." This essay summarizes some recent research findings that touch on the issues explored in the cases of *Making Meaning for Operations*.

By focusing on central mathematical concepts across the grades, Developing Mathematical Ideas modules support teachers in understanding how these ideas develop and what they look like as students grapple with aspects of these ideas in a variety of problem contexts. It is not enough for teachers to know only the core work of their own grade levels. First, any classroom will include students who are working in a range of different places in their own understanding. Teachers also need to recognize how students might be building ideas expected before their grade level as well as toward those that follow. Second, teachers themselves should develop as deep and complete an understanding of these concepts as possible—both for their own learning and as a basis for making instructional judgments.

Developing Mathematical Ideas (DMI) was intentionally developed to support the concrete coherence and focus in the professional development of teachers of the elementary and middle grades to which the *Common Core State Standards for Mathematics* (CCSSM) aspires. Focus is provided by the selection for each DMI module of core mathematical ideas that underlie a key segment of mathematics content, while coherence comes from the careful analysis of how these core ideas connect to each other and are developed and applied by students across the grades. DMI is designed to help teachers understand these core ideas more deeply for themselves and to gain extensive knowledge about how students engage with the progression of these ideas.

The material of this module is the substance of the CCSSM domains Operations and Algebraic Thinking (K–4) and Number and Operations—Fractions (3–5), which develop a progression of understanding the operations with whole numbers from kindergarten to grade 4 and expanding that understanding to include fractions, starting in grade 3.

Although all of the Standards for Mathematical Practice (SMP) are illustrated in this module, two of them are emphasized: practice 2, reason abstractly and quantitatively and practice 3, construct viable arguments and critique the reasoning of others. Practice 2 is a focus of the work throughout the module. Reasoning abstractly and quantitatively has to do with decontextualizing problems expressed as situations and contextualizing problems expressed numerically. That is, a central part of understanding the meaning of the operations is being able to see how that meaning is expressed as relationships or actions on quantities in a context, how the meaning is expressed with numbers and symbols, and how to move fluidly between the two. As students describe the relationship between symbols and context, they are often also engaged in practice 3, constructing and critiquing arguments about the quantities in a problem and the nature of the result. In addition, practice 1, make sense of problems and persevere in solving them, is central to the work of all of the DMI modules. Throughout the *Making Meaning for Operations* seminar, you will have opportunities to discuss and reflect on how the Standards of Mathematical Practice appear in the sessions.

When this DMI seminar was first taught, many seminar participants reported that they had to learn how to read the cases:

> "It's different from reading a story. I feel as if I've had to read through each episode with a fine-tooth comb."

> "I'm reading cases very slowly, and I'm writing down thoughts about what I'm seeing in the text."

"I find that when I do the mathematics problems that the students in the case are working on, I can better understand what they are doing."

Other participants offered advice to future seminar attendees:

"Read all the cases in a chapter once and try to write down the mathematical issues they raise. You might focus attention on two or three children that interest you and really figure out the mathematical issues that these few children are facing. Try to really understand how the children are thinking. Here's another way to do it: After reading all the cases in a chapter, go over them again, looking for common threads. What mathematical issues connect these cases together?"

"Remember that these are glimpses of real kids dealing with real situations, struggling to make sense of very difficult concepts. Pay particular attention to the natural ways students often solve problems."

"Begin with the chapter introduction, which alerts you to the ideas you should pay attention to."

"If possible, discuss the cases informally with other participants before the sessions. If you're unable to do any or some of the above, by all means, still come to the seminar!"

As the seminar proceeds, you might talk to other participants about the ways they read the cases to prepare for seminar discussions

Making meaning for whole number addition and subtraction

As you read the following word problems, consider for a moment which of the operations—addition, subtraction, multiplication, or division—you would use to find the answer to each one.

There are 13 insects in front of us on the paper and 5 spiders behind my back. What is the total number of insects and spiders?

There are 10 girls in our class, and 8 of them are here today. How many girls are out today?

We can easily identify the operations that would give us the answers: addition ($13 + 5 = 18$) and subtraction ($10 - 8 = 2$). But what is it that children must understand to solve these story problems? What happens when such problems are posed to children who have not yet learned symbols for the operations and have not yet learned their arithmetic facts? How do children find answers to such problems when they haven't yet learned to add or subtract? The first three cases of this chapter allow us to examine these questions. As you read these cases, take notes on the following questions:

• What do we learn about the operations while following the counting strategies that young children use to solve problems and by pondering the confusions that arise for them?

• What do we learn about the ideas that children must put together in order for them to develop an understanding of the operations?

In the remaining cases in this chapter (cases 4 through 7), we meet students who have developed some ideas about addition and subtraction and can solve problems using these operations. However, the questions they ask, the confusions they hold, and the insights they offer reveal the greater complexity underlying what may seem to be very basic concepts. One set of questions involves mathematical issues for you:

• Can a single situation be modeled by different operations?

• Can a single operation model different kinds of actions?

• What can we see about the operations through different representations such as cubes and number lines?

A second set of questions prompts us to consider the children's processes of putting ideas together:

• In these samples from grades 1–7, what can be observed about the ways in which students' ideas develop?

• What appear to be some of the difficulties students face as they learn about addition and subtraction?

• How can different representations support students' understanding of addition and subtraction?

As you read the cases, take notes on these questions. Then, after reading the cases, review the questions again.

case 1

Insects and spiders and counting on

Dan
GRADE 1, SEPTEMBER

As part of our science study of insects and spiders, the children sorted small plastic models onto two large sheets of paper labeled "Insects" and "Spiders." As they placed their figures, they had to tell what attributes they were using to make their decisions. After we sorted the models and confirmed that each was in the correct set, I asked, "How many insects are there?"

The insects were positioned randomly on the sheet. I called on Mike. As he counted the insects, his finger jumped around from one to another, making it difficult to keep track of which ones he had counted and which he had missed. He ended up miscounting by one, coming up with 14. Some children said they disagreed with his count. 5

I next asked Annie to count the insects. Although she didn't count them in an easily discernible order (e.g., left to right, or top to bottom, or by moving them as she counted), she was clearly able to keep track because she did not recount or leave out any insects. She came up with the correct answer of 13. 10

I asked one more child, Renaldo, to count to see whether his answer would agree with either of the previous answers or would be completely different. He counted the insects in an organized way: as he said each number, he moved one item into a group of already counted insects. He came up with 13, just as Annie did. 15

I asked the group, "Why did we get different answers, 14 and 13?" Renaldo quickly replied that Mike had "counted too many." Nods from many of the children seemed to suggest agreement. I think he meant that Mike had counted some insect or insects more than once. Because the children seemed content with Renaldo's response, I assumed they agreed that 13 was the answer and did not pursue this question any further. 20

The children were quickly able to see that there were only 5 spiders on the other sheet. Because we had not counted the total number of insects and spiders, I decided to find out how the children would determine how many there were altogether if I removed the 5 spiders from view. How would they solve the problem? How would they represent items that were absent and keep them in the count? Would they start at 13 or at 1 to get the new count? 25

After I put the spiders behind my back I said, "If we know that there are 13 insects and that there are 5 spiders to be added, how many would there be altogether?"

Lindsey immediately raised her hand and answered 18. She explained that she thought of 13 insects in her head and counted on 5 more spiders in her head. 30

Then I called on Mike. He recounted the 13 insects very carefully, one by one (in contrast to his earlier somewhat careless, random counting), and then touched and counted 5 imaginary spiders with one hand while raising 5 fingers, one at a time, on his other hand. Like Lindsey, he also came up with 18.

Liliana took a different approach. She counted the 13 insects and then separated 5 from that group and counted them on from the 13, also ending up with 18.

I brought the 5 spiders into view and together we all counted the 13 insects and 5 spiders to confirm that there really were 18.

These three students seem to represent a developmental sequence that children may go through in becoming comfortable with adding quantities together. Liliana started from 1, counted the 13 visible insects, and then separated 5 from that group as a concrete way to keep track of the additional 5 that she was counting. Mike seemed to be less dependent on the concrete objects. He also started at 1 with the 13 insects, but then counted the additional 5 by touching imaginary spiders with one hand while keeping track with 5 fingers on his other hand. He seemed to have internalized that there are a total of 5 fingers on one of his hands as he did not count them out before counting them on. It did not seem to be a problem for him that his fingers could be labeled "1, 2, 3, 4, 5" in one situation and "14, 15, 16, 17, 18" in another situation. Liliana and Mike either did not recognize or did not trust that the 13 previously counted insects would still be 13, or they could not comfortably start counting in the middle of the number sequence. Lindsey, by contrast, clearly trusted that the new number included the original 13 and didn't feel a need to start counting from 1. She seemed able to visualize a group that she could label 13 plus 5 more individual spiders that she could easily count on in her head.

I wondered if the children had a sense of the commutative property of addition, and decided to investigate. Would they recognize that we would get the same answer whether we began with the 5 and added on 13 or started with 13 and added on 5?

I put the 13 insects behind my back, showed the children the 5 spiders, and asked how many there would be altogether if I were to add in the missing 13. Many of the children immediately said 18. I raised the question, "How do you know it is the same answer?" Although I can't recall a clear answer from anyone, they gave variations on knowing that there were still 13 insects and we had already counted 5 spiders. I asked if there was any way that we could count them all up by first using the 5 spiders that we could see. No one responded.

Did these children really understand the commutative property for addition? Or was the answer easy for them because there were no new variables—that is, there were still 13 insects and 5 spiders? Even though I had changed the placement of each, the children may not have seen this as a different situation. Would they have said so quickly that the answer was still 18 if I had changed or eliminated a defining variable, for example, if the 13 and the 5 were all insects?

I tried a problem with different numbers to see how they would deal with adding on a missing number of items that was more than 10: "What if I told you there were 11 insects to add to the 5 spiders we already have in front of us?" Liliana counted the 5 spiders that she saw. Then, without counting out ten fingers beforehand, she continued counting on her fingers one at a time to 15, and said she needed 1 more to make 16.

I found it interesting that Liliana was not daunted by the fact that she had only ten fingers. She seemed to have internalized that all her fingers always make a group called "10" and 1 more finger makes another group called "11." In addition, Liliana seemed comfortable with the fact that her ten fingers could be called "1, 2, 3, 4, 5, 6, 7, 8, 9, 10" in one situation and "6, 7, 8, 9, 10, 11, 12, 13, 14, 15" in another.

To verify that the children understood the importance of one-to-one correspondence in counting, I added 11 insects to the group of 5 spiders. I counted the 5 carefully, and then I continued to count the extra 11 insects randomly until I was way into the 20s. Many of the children shouted "No!" and said I could only count each insect once. Renaldo recounted for the group, carefully moving and placing each one into a new group of already-counted insects. He got 16, confirming Liliana's answer.

Many of the children seem to understand the need for one-to-one correspondence and for only counting each item one time so that you get a specific answer that is repeatable. Many may have some sense of the commutative property for addition, but I cannot be sure of this without further investigation. Some of them clearly understand that a group of items has a constant value even when another group is added to them, and that it is not necessary to start over from 1 when adding the new items on one by one; others do not have this awareness or trust yet. Some interesting questions come up:

• When do children move from merely counting to actually understanding addition?

• Is it when they can count on from a number rather than having to start again from 1?

• Or can children who have to start at 1 every time still understand that they are adding and not just counting?

case 2

Going up and down with numbers

Wendy
KINDERGARTEN, MARCH

As we start each day in kindergarten, we assemble at the rug area for our opening meeting. One   95
of the things we discuss is the number of children in school. This morning, as usual, we counted
the number of boys, which today totaled 9, and then the number of girls, which totaled 8. I
wrote on the board:

9 boys

8 girls   100

I then asked, "How many boys are out today?"

Natalie raised her hand and answered, "When all the boys are here, we have 10 boys, so
today we have 9 boys, so 1 boy is out."

"How many girls are out today?"

Peter raised his hand and said, "It's 2." He knew that there were 10 girls in the class when   105
all were present.

I asked, "How did you figure it out?"

Peter replied, "8 and 1 and . . . " He seemed to be stuck in his thinking. I feel he did figure
it out correctly, but then had trouble explaining.

I then asked, "Can someone else tell me how many girls are out today?"   110

Denisha's hand went up. She said, "It's 2, because 8 is 2 numbers down from 10."

"What does that mean?" I asked Denisha.

"When all the girls are here, it's 10," she told us. "You go down from 10 by 1, that's 9, and
down 1 more, that's 8, so that's 2."

We usually count around the circle to find the total number in class for the day. I decided   115
instead to see if the children could come up with the total just by looking at the numbers.

9 boys

8 girls

"How many kids here today?" I asked. Daniel answered, "17."

I said, "Daniel, if you look at the numbers of boys and girls, can you tell me how you got   120
17?" He didn't reply. I think that Daniel counted around the circle and didn't want to tell me
that.

Rachelle offered, "8 and 9 makes a 1 and a 7." When I asked Rachelle how she knew that,
she answered, "I counted in my mind."

"How did you count in your mind? Say it out loud."   125

She began, "1, 2, 3, 4, 5, 6, 7, 8, 9 . . . " But she didn't go on. She wasn't using her fingers, so I'm not sure how she was going to explain the answer.

"Did anyone else figure it out in a different way?" I wondered. Tamara's hand went up and she said, "It's 17, 8 and 9. Take 1 away from the 9 that makes it an 8, and 8 and 8 makes 16. So you put the 9 back. You go up one more from 8, you make a 9 and you have the 8, you get 17. You're going one more higher than 16." 130

I was amazed at how several of the children could see the relationship that numbers have to each other. They used the phrase "going up or down" to describe this. Tamara "went down" one from the 9 to make 8. It seemed easier for her to add 8 and 8, yet she knew that 9 was one more than 8 so the 16 had to "go up" by one. I feel that Peter was thinking about "going up" when he said 8 and 1, but couldn't say the one more to make 10. Denisha described "going down" from 10 by one, and by one again to get 8. She then knew 2 girls were absent. Being able to go up and down with numbers seems to be a key to understanding number differences. 135

138

case 3

Complexities of counting back

Denise
GRADE 2, OCTOBER

For the past year I've been interested in the ways second graders come to understand addition, subtraction, and regrouping. I've watched children invent methods that reflect a tremendous amount of what I term "sophistication" and flexibility in how they think about numbers. Among the "least sophisticated" methods for subtracting that I identified were kids counting backwards on their fingers or collecting a quantity of counters, say 22, for example, and then taking away 5.

I am also intrigued by how kids move toward increasingly sophisticated and flexible thinking about number. In the first couple of weeks of school, I actively watched for examples that would help me begin to illuminate something (who knows just what?) about number sense. What I found was a surprise. I'm very interested in hearing if anyone is similarly puzzled, grabbed, or surprised by this event!

The activity we were working on is called "Enough for the Class" (from *Counting, Coins, and Combinations* in the curriculum *Investigations in Number, Data, and Space*, 2nd ed., Pearson Learning, 2008). I show my class a bag of cubes and tell them we need to figure out if there are enough cubes in the bag for everyone to take one. If there are too many or too few, how many too many or too few are there?

As a class we counted the cubes in the bag and found that there were 32. We had 25 students in our class that day.

I witnessed students solving this problem in a variety of ways. Some solved it by adding on their fingers from 25 to 32 and getting 7. Others solved it by counting backwards from 32 until they got to 25. Others saw that by adding 5 to 25 they got to 30 quickly, and then added 2 more to the 5. Some solved it with cubes stacked to a length of 32, taking off cubes until there were 25.

Susan counted backwards and recorded her method on her paper like this: 32 | | | | | | 25. She got 6 for her answer.

The next day when we discussed different students' methods, there was general agreement that 7 was the answer. I called on Susan, hoping she'd talk about her method. Instead, she used a strip of 32 cubes that a classmate had just used. She took off 7 cubes one by one and indeed got 25. (I was a little disappointed; I had hoped she would bring her method to the class.) Then her face looked puzzled and she said, "But I remember yesterday I got 6."

I said, "But today you got 7. Hmm. How could that be?"

Susan repeated her process with 32 cubes, recounting to be sure there were really 32 cubes in her strip and then carefully taking off 7 and recounting those remaining 25 cubes again. She was very puzzled.

Other students restated their process that gave them the answer 7, and Susan was still puzzled. I asked her to look again at her paper and reminded her, "Didn't you count backwards, Susan?"

Susan looked at her work from the previous day more closely. "Oh yes, I did."   175

I drew on the board Susan's figure from yesterday, 32 | | | | | | 25, and said, "This is what Susan drew. There's the 6."

Some children said, "Yeah, there's 6."

This was a genuine confusion for a few minutes as students buzzed about how they had got 7, but here was Susan getting 6 one way and 7 another.   180

In a few seconds Clara said, "Well, Susan has to take away either the 32 or the 25 in order to get 7." I said, "Right, but why?"

Several other children offered up how and why 7 was in fact the answer. They pointed out that with 32 cubes, you are taking away the 32nd cube, the 31st cube, the 30th cube, the 29th, the 28th, the 27th, and the 26th cube, and then you are left with 25 cubes.   185

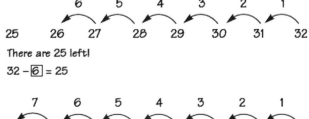

But when you count backwards on your fingers or out loud, you start at 32 and don't count 1 until you get to 31, then 2 is at 30, 3 is at 29, 4 is at 28, 5 is at 27, 6 is at 26, and when you count back the 7th time, you get to 25.   190

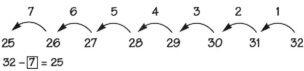

Drawing these diagrams myself much later highlighted the complexities in a method I had always assumed was "less sophisticated." Indeed, this counting backwards does seem simple at first glance. But, if I didn't know already that 32 take away 7 is 25, how would I construct and   195
make sense of the difference between these two ways of thinking? In my quest to investigate number sense and to identify how children develop it, this moment really sits with me still.

 In fact, this issue came up several weeks later when we were considering how many kids are here in class if 4 of them are absent. Ricky reasoned similarly to Susan's first assertion in my earlier example, that starting at 26 . . . 25 (1) . . . 24 (2) . . . 23 (3) . . . 22 (4), and there's 21   200
left. So there must be 21 kids here.

Many children spoke up quickly and heatedly, insisting that they knew 22 plus 4 is 26, and so if there are 4 kids not here, there must be 22 here. Others clamored that Ricky had to take away the 26 first or that he got to 22 as he took away the 4th kid. Many of my students are quite convinced and clear about how they would take 4 away from 26. Ricky and Susan have simply piqued my interest about how they will become convinced, now that I consider some of the complexities of what might or might not happen in their construct.

205

207

case 4

Missing part versus missing change

Kina
GRADE 1, JANUARY

I went over to work with Zenobia on a story problem because she looked horribly confused. This was the problem: 210

Max had 3 blocks. He found some more blocks. Then he had 7 blocks. How many blocks did he find?

Zenobia had 3 cubes and 7 cubes and wasn't sure what to do. She counted all of them and got 10, but she looked at me with confusion and said, "I know that's not the answer."

We acted out the problem (or rather, I acted it out). I said, "Max had 3 blocks. Here are the   215
3 blocks. Then he found some. Oh, look, here are some more blocks. Now he has 7 blocks. So he had 3, got some more, and both of those together made 7, right?"

Zenobia looked at me, and I could tell that she was trying to understand it, but it was just too much. So I said, "If you're still not sure you understand, it is OK to say, 'I'm still confused.'"

She said, "I'm still confused."   220

Then I wondered if making a connection to something more familiar would help her, so I brought her back to another activity, one at which she is routinely successful. I said, "Let's put this aside for a moment and solve another problem. Pretend that you and I are playing 'How Many Am I Hiding?' We're playing with 6 cubes. I have some behind my back. You can see 2. You know that there are 6 cubes all together. How many am I hiding?"   225

Zenobia thought and said, "4."

I asked, "Does it remind you of anything we've just been doing?" Zenobia replied, "Not really."

I said, "OK, then let's pretend that Max was playing 'How Many Am I Hiding?' He could see 3. Some were behind his friend's back. He knew the total was 7. How many were hiding?"   230

Zenobia thought and then said, "4."

I asked, "OK, so do you see any connections between this problem and the other Max problem?"

She said, "Yes, there's a 3 and a 7. I just don't get it, still."

After that, Zenobia and I took a break from the problem. Sometimes you spend so much time   235
on something that it just becomes too much. So she went to work on some other math problems.

For me, the connection between the story problem and the "How Many Am I Hiding?" game seems so obvious. What is the connection Zenobia needs to make? And what about her classmates? I am thinking about how to start a class discussion to see what ideas students might have about the connections between the game and the story problems.   240

case 5

Valentine stickers

Jody
GRADES 1 AND 2, JANUARY

When the children arrive each morning, right away they start work on the problem of the day, which I have written on a chart or on the board. One day last week, I had this word problem displayed:

> Sabrina and Yvonne have 14 stickers when they put their stickers together. 245
> Yvonne has 6 stickers. How many stickers does Sabrina have?

Solving the problem of the day has become a routine in my class; after settling in, the children just go and get any materials they need (cubes, links, counters) to solve the problem. They know that they have to keep a record of their strategies for solving the problem, using models, pictures, words, or number sentences, so they would be able to explain their thinking 250 process to someone else.

This is how Latasha, a first grader, solved the problem. First she drew 14 hearts on her paper. Then she wrote numbers 1 to 6 inside the first 6 hearts. Then she started again, writing from 1 to 8 on the remaining hearts. She marked off the first 6 hearts. Below her picture of hearts, she wrote 6 + 8 = 14. 255

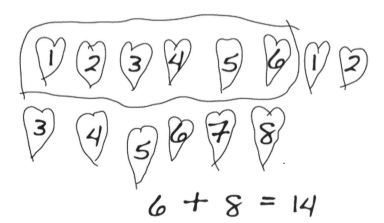

Most adults would think of this as a subtraction problem, but Latasha represented it with an addition sentence. When I saw what she was doing, I wanted to make sure that she was clear about her process and that she understood the problem. I asked Latasha what was the 14. She 260 said that this was the number of stickers Sabrina and Yvonne had together. When I asked her how many stickers Sabrina had, she quickly pointed to the hearts labeled 1 to 8 that she had not put a circle around and said, "Sabrina has 8 stickers." Her responses assured me that she understood what the problem was and that her strategy was clear to her.

Jessie, a second grader, did not draw a picture for this problem. Instead she wrote the following on her paper:

> If Yvonne has 6 stickers and they have 14 altogether, I figured it out by minusing 6 from 14.

> $14 - 6 = 8$

> I also figured it out like this:

> $6 + \_\_\_ = 14$

> I know that $6 + 6 = 12$, add 2 more $= 14$, so $6 + 8 = 14$

Having known Jessie for more than a year, since she was in my first-grade class last year, I know that she feels comfortable explaining her thinking process using numbers. Sometimes she uses pictures or other representations, but for this particular problem she didn't, and I felt she understood the problem. Jessie is used to explaining different ways of solving a problem. The numbers involved in the problem were low enough that she could visualize them without using objects or pictures. She knows her number combinations, and she was able to solve the problem with both addition and subtraction. She also used what she knows about doubles to get her answer.

Cecile, another second grader, did not use pictures or objects either. She explained her method like this:

I know that $7 + 7 = 14$, so I took 1 from one of the 7s and put it on the other 7 so now it is $6 + 8$ and it's 14.

I asked Cecile what she was thinking when she started with $7 + 7 = 14$. She said, "$7 + 7$ is easier for me to think about and that makes 14, so if I move 1 from one of the 7s to the other, I have $6 + 8$ and that is 14." When I asked her how many stickers Sabrina has, she said, "8."

Cecile feels comfortable with renaming addends that add up to the same number. One of our daily routines is thinking of many different ways to rename a number using doubles, addition, and subtraction. Cecile often thinks of numbers that are easier and more convenient for her to deal with to help her solve problems.

Maya is a first grader. For the sticker problem, she took 14 cubes and made a tower. Then she took 6 cubes and made another tower. She lined up the two towers next to each other, like this:

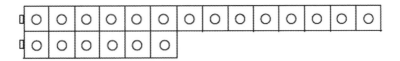

When she counted how many cubes there were beyond her 6-cube tower, she found that there were 8.

When I saw what Maya had done, I was struck by the fact that her model consisted of more than 14 cubes. I asked her what the 8 cubes represented, and she said it was Sabrina's stickers. She said that the 6-cube tower below the 14-cube tower was only a way for her to remember how many stickers Yvonne had. She was using the extra 6 cubes as a marker so she could easily see how many stickers Sabrina had. I then asked her what the 14 cubes represented, and she said that these were the stickers that Yvonne and Sabrina had together. Maya could explain her process clearly by using objects, but when I asked her if she could tell me a math sentence that showed what she had just done, she was not able to do it.

Joachim, a second grader, had drawn this on his paper:

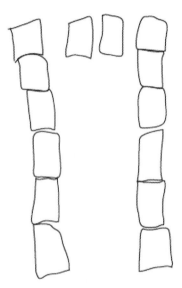

Joachim's model confused me at first, so I asked him to explain his process. This is what he said: "I took 2 sixes and added them. That is 12. But this is not the correct number, so I added 2 to the 12, and it is 14. So now it is $6 + 6 + 2 = 14$. And $6 + 8 = 14$."

Joachim's way is similar to Cecile's. They both relied on their knowledge of doubles to get to the right number.

I asked Damien, who had chosen to use a number strip, how he solved the problem. He put his finger on 6 and said, "I started counting up from 6 until I got to 14, and I counted 8." As I listened to him count, he said "1" as he pointed to 7, "2" as he pointed to 8, and kept moving up until he said "8" as he pointed to 14. Damien also made 14 circles on his paper and counted off 6 by putting a line across each of 6 circles. There were 8 circles left.

6   8

Antoinette used cubes to help her solve the problem. She explained her process like this: 320
"Since Yvonne has 6 stickers, I took 6 cubes. Then I said, how many more cubes should I take to get to 14, and then I counted up until I got to 14, and there were 8 more."

When I asked Antoinette to show me how she counted up from 6, she said, "6 … [pause], 7, 8, 9, 10, 11, 12, 13, 14." Her way of solving the problem is similar to Damien's first way. Although they had different materials, both used counting up to solve the problem.   325

Kim, a second grader, and Dylan, a first grader, were working together and role-playing the problem, pretending that one of them was Yvonne and the other was Sabrina. They counted 14 teddy bear counters together. Then Kim said, "I am Yvonne and you are Sabrina. I have 6 teddy bears. How many teddy bears do you have?" Dylan, acting as Sabrina, counted his teddy bears and exclaimed, "I have 8. So Sabrina has 8 stickers!" They were having a good time pretending,   330
and when I left them, I asked them to try to think of another way to solve the same problem.

All the children had appropriate solution methods, and used methods they were familiar with. Some used number combinations that were easy for them to think about. They understood the problem and were able to explain their strategies and represent the problem in different ways. My goal for all my students is that they feel comfortable in communicating their thinking process   335
while also expanding their repertoire of strategies for problem solving. I encourage them to try solving a problem in more than one way and to share their strategies with someone else. I would also like my students to explore the properties of addition and subtraction. Jessie, who used the operations, knew that the problem could be solved by either addition or subtraction.   339

case 6

Finding the difference: Should I add or subtract?

Machiko
GRADE 4, NOVEMBER

My students had been exploring the relationship between addition and subtraction for several   340
weeks. They had worked with related problems such as 125 + 34 = ____ and 159 − ____ = 34. We
had also been exploring the meaning of the equals sign with problems such as 74 + 22 =
80 + ____. I was interested in finding out how they might apply the ideas and strategies they
were developing to a problem that asked them to consider the difference between two numbers.

What does "difference" mean?   345

I offered the class the following problem to think about:

Find two numbers whose difference is 153.

After a few minutes of watching their individual work, I realized I needed to bring the class
together to talk about what it meant to find the difference between two numbers. I said, "As I
walked around, I noticed that you were approaching the problem in many ways. I am wondering   350
what you all are thinking about. What do you think it means to find the difference?"

Chloe:	It's what you get when you add.
Trey:	I think that's the sum.
Alex:	It's when you subtract.
Katie:	On the number line, it's how far apart two numbers are; I think they meant to 355 write the distance.

I asked Katie if she could show us what she meant. She came up to the number line we have
posted on our wall and pointed to 10 and then 20, saying, "These are 10 away from each other."
Then Tara chimed in.

Tara:	The 20 is 10 away from 30. 360
Teacher:	We can say that 20 is 10 away from 30, and we can also say that the difference between 20 and 30 is 10.
Joe:	[*coming up to the number line and pointing at 30*] And the difference between 30 and 40 is 10!
Katie:	I just put 0 in the calculator and then added 153, and I got 153. If I put in a 365 number and add 153 to it, I get a number that would be 153 more.

Teacher:	How could we use Katie's idea to find more numbers that have a difference of 153?
Katie:	I can make a pattern now. [*She comes to the board and writes.*]

$$1 + 153 = 154$$
$$2 + 153 = 155$$

370

I was unsure whether the class was relating the addend to which 153 was being added and the resulting sum as having a difference of 153. I wondered if using an unmarked number line might highlight the idea of the difference between two numbers. How would the students connect Katie's addition equations to the placement of the numbers and the distance between those numbers on a number line? Would they recognize a similar subtraction problem that could be modeled by the same numbers on a number line?

375

Since a few students had already used our posted number line to talk about differences of 10, I said, "A few minutes ago, Joe and Katie came up and showed us numbers that were 10 apart, or had a difference of 10, on the number line. I wonder what the numbers Katie has written on the board would look like on a number line."

380

Reesa enthusiastically volunteered to come up and show her thinking. She drew the following number line:

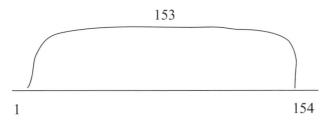

Reesa:	You start at 1, and then you hop 153 to land on 154.	385
Teacher:	So, how does what Reesa drew on the board help us find two numbers whose difference is 153?
Leana:	See, the 1 plus the hop of 153 is 154.
Joe:	Oh … the 1 is 153 different than the 154.
Alex:	We can put the 2 on the row.	390
Teacher:	What are you thinking about, Alex?
Alex:	Put the 2 on the line, and also put the 153.
Trey:	But the 153 is the jump. We need to put 155.
Tessa:	And then put a 3 and a 156!

Lots of voices started offering comments, and many thumbs were up requesting airtime. I asked the class to talk in their small groups about what they were noticing and thinking. As

395

I walked around, students were continuing Katie's pattern in their math journals and talking about how they would place the numbers on the number line. Were they noticing that each time they came up with two new numbers, those numbers were the same distance apart on the number line? 400

The number line seemed to allow the students to form a visual image for the pattern Katie had offered. They were now exploring a method for finding many pairs of numbers with a difference of 153. After a few minutes, we came back together to discuss what ideas were developing.

Teacher:	What are some ideas or questions your group talked about?
Trey:	Why are we adding 153? I thought we should subtract it. 405

There was no response to his question! A few seconds of silence and confused looks followed. I was glad for the wait time as I was thinking about where his question might now lead the discussion.

Chloe:	[*pointing to Katie's addition sentences*] Yeah, this isn't subtraction.
Brad:	When we're jumping on the number line, we're adding 153. 410
Leana:	I took a number and took away 153. That is subtracting.
Trey:	But Katie added.
Emily:	I think it works both ways. We can add or subtract.
Joe:	Add or subtract what?
Teacher:	How about if we pick a number and try out your ideas? 415
Alex:	Let's use 77.

Emily came up to the board and drew a new number line.

That she had placed 77 in the middle of the line intrigued me. But before I could ask her about her representation, Donny spoke up, saying "Add 153 like Katie did." 420
Donny came up and made a jump of 153, landing on 230.

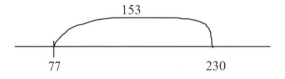

The class decided to check 77 + 153 on the calculator.

Emily:	So 77 is 153 away from 230, but why did he add? 425

Alex:	Because the difference means one is more than the other, and the 230 is 153 more.
Teacher:	230 is 153 more than what?
Brad:	Than 77. So if we add 153 to a number, we get one number that is 153 more than the other number.
Toshana:	Yes, you can see it here [*pointing to the jump of 153 on the line*].
Leana:	Remember, I subtracted.
Teacher:	Leana, show us how you subtracted.

430

Leana came to the number line, and starting at 230, showed a jump backward of 153 to land on 77.

Alex:	You can subtract or add 153. Those two are basically the same: $1 + 153 = 154$ and $154 - 153 = 1$.

435

Throughout the small- and whole-group discussions, the students had been moving back and forth between addition and subtraction as they thought about the difference between two numbers. I was intrigued by the way the numbers they chose affected their thinking about the relationship between the operations of addition and subtraction.

440

Teacher:	How many numbers do you think have a difference of 153?
Tessa:	A lot of numbers, because you can add lots of numbers to get 153. Like $150 + 3$, or $151 + 2$.
Alex:	But those don't have a difference of 153; they equal 153.
Tessa:	Oh, those are combinations that equal 153.
Alex:	I think there are all the numbers that you can add to 153. They will never end.
Teacher:	Let's think about Tessa's idea of adding numbers that equal 153. Are there any numbers that we can add, and those numbers will still have a difference of 153?
Katie:	Only 0!
Donny:	Because $0 + 153$ equals 153, and you would have to hop 153 from 0 to get to 153.

445

450

Subtracting a greater number from a lesser number

Alex took us back to the number line on which Donny had showed $77 + 153 = 230$.

Alex:	We can also subtract 153 from 77.
Teacher:	Can we show that on the number line we have up here?
Donny:	No, because it will go past the 0. Then it won't be 153 away.
Alex:	Yes, we can, but it will be negative.

455

Teacher:	So, do you all want to try and subtract to see what happens?
Brad:	Yes, let's jump the other way!
Emily:	I think we will land on negative 230, because now we are subtracting.

Brad came up and made a jump of 153 to the left of the 77.

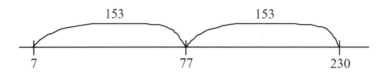

Joe:	What are we going to put there?
Toshana:	I subtracted 153 − 77 on the calculator and I got 76.
Tessa:	I subtracted 77 − 153 and I got a minus 76.
Alex:	You can subtract 153 from a bigger number, like 179, but not from smaller numbers.
Emily:	You can use smaller numbers than 153, but you will go into the negative.
Brad:	And you can subtract or add.
Chloe:	We can write 77 + 153 or 77 − 153?
Reesa:	You can do either one.
Alex:	I can show the other hop on the number line. We already figured out that 77 − 153 is minus 76 on the calculator.

Alex then came up and made a hop to 0 and then a hop to –76. It was interesting that he had stopped at 0 before he hopped to –76. I wondered if the class was thinking about what the distances of the two smaller hops were.

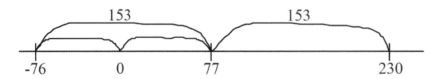

Teacher:	What is the difference between 77 and 0?

I heard many voices call out 77. Donny asked if he could put a 77 on the hop. After he recorded that on the board, I continued by asking, "What about the small hop that is left?"

Tessa:	77.
Chloe:	76.
Donny:	It has to be 76, because 76 + 77 is 153.
Alex:	The two hops have to be the same as the big hop of 153.

460

465

470

475

480

485

Assessing what students learned

A few days later, I offered students two new problems:

Find two numbers whose difference is 58.

Find two numbers whose difference is 134.

Much of their work indicated that an unmarked number line was an integral part of their strate-   490
gies. Figures 1.1 to 1.5 are representative of the work of the class.

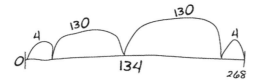

Fig. 1.1. Donny uses 134 as a starting number to find numbers that have a difference of 134.

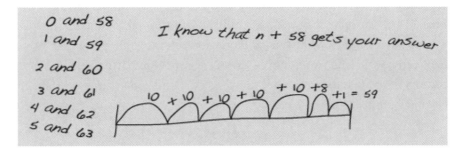

Fig. 1.2. Reesa finds pairs of numbers that have a difference of 58.   495

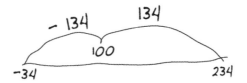

Fig. 1.3. Brad represents two numbers that have a difference of 134 from 100.

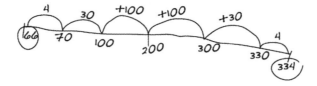

Fig. 1.4. Katie represents two numbers that have a difference of 134 from 200.

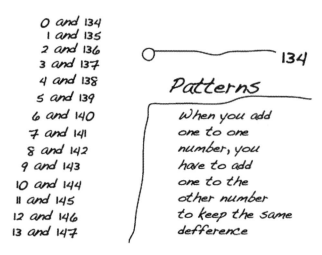

Fig. 1.5. Alex uses a pattern to find many pairs of numbers with a difference of 134.

I was left reflecting on the students' variety of strategies for thinking about the difference between two numbers. How do students develop a multifaceted meaning for a word like "difference"? How was the relationship between addition and subtraction highlighted for students as they explored how to find two numbers that have a specified difference?

   Would they have observed that the difference could be either an addend or a subtrahend without the models of the number lines?

case 7

Number line models for subtraction

Carl
GRADE 7, JUNE

We are coming to the end of another school year and I am thinking about the importance of models for student learning in mathematics. Students in my classes have used balance models   510
for equations; rectangle and groups-of-groups models for the distributive property; number line, chip, and savings-debt models for operations with negative numbers; and tables, graphs, equations, and walking-rate models for understanding linear relationships. Models help students make sense of mathematical ideas in a way that connects to their own understanding. Without models, students are dependent on the teacher- or text-provided algorithms, which may or may   515
not make sense to them. With models, students can use the contextual clues of the materials or situation to help them sort out and justify effective versus invalid strategies and ideas.

I decided to take students back to a basic operation to see how they would now use a model to make sense of that operation. I assigned two problems, asking students to use a number line to show how they thought about and solved them.   520

1. I have $465. I spend $180 on video games. How much money do I have left for my trip to Hawaii?

2. I am taking a trip to visit a friend in another state. I drive 180 miles and then stop to rest. The total distance to my friend's house is 465 miles. How much farther do I have to go?   525

The take-away strategy was by far the most prevalent approach for problem 1. With this strategy, students would start at 465 on the number line and then go back (left) 180 units toward 0. They used a variety of methods to do this. Howard showed an arching line from 465 to 365, then another arching line from 365 to 300, and finally an arching line from 300 to 285. I asked him to explain this and he said, "465 minus 100 is 365, and 365 minus 65 is 300. I have used up   530
165 of 180, so I need 15 more to use up all 180."

Tina showed arching lines of 20 each to get from 465 back to 285.

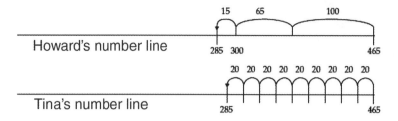

Fig. 1.6. Two number line approaches to problem 1

The adding-up, or difference-between, strategy was by far the most prevalent approach for problem 2. Mark put a big dot at 180 and at 465. He then showed arching lines from 180 to 200, 200 to 400, and 400 to 465. Above these lines he wrote the number 285. Denali's diagram looked similar, but he had arching lines that went 10 at a time from 180 to 460. Then he added another 5.

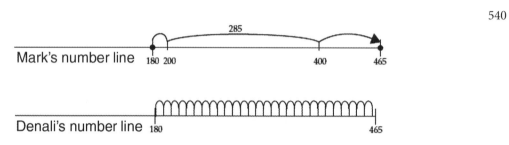

Fig. 1.7. Two number-line approaches to problem 2

I asked the class why most of them had used take-away for the first problem and some other method for the second problem.

Alexis explained, "In the first problem, you have some money and you are giving it to the cashier. With the second problem, you want to know how far it is from one place to another. They just feel different."

Ian added, "It's like looking on a map. With the second problem, you're looking at a map that shows where you are and where you are going. You want to know how far that is."

The explanations of Alexis and Ian highlight how a model can influence the action a student sees in a problem. Different strategies can feel like a better match for one kind of action than another. In the first problem, the context conveys an action of taking away. I have some money and then money is taken away. The number line approach of starting at 465 and working back feels more consistent. In the second problem, the context conveys the idea of finding the distance between. Putting marks at 180 and 465 and finding what lies between feels more like how people use a map, which is what students would use for a car trip.

I am now wondering what this difference in strategies means to these seventh graders. Do they see these as the same operation, or do they view them as different operations? How do they

535

540

545

550

555

make sense of take-away strategies and adding-up strategies representing the same problem of 465 – 180? If I asked them to write a number sentence for both of these problems, would they write 465 – 180 = 285 for both, or would they write 180 + n = 465 for the second? 560

All year long we have been using fact families to help us with operations involving decimals, fractions, and negative numbers. Do they see the connection of these two problems to fact families? I also wonder what kind of instructional moves would help students make and leverage these connections. I can see them, but do they? What kinds of classroom discussions move this beyond simply solving two different problems to deepening their understanding of subtraction? 565

Although the two strategies described were the most common, students also used strategies that took advantage of other ideas we had worked with during the year. Negative number strategies came up in a couple of different ways. For problem 1, Akeem started his number line at negative 180 and then showed an arching line going up 465 to positive 285. At first, I 570 thought he had completely abandoned the context of the problem and created a problem that he knew gave the same answer. When I asked him how his model fit the context, he said, "My dad usually pays for the stuff with his credit card and I pay him back. I would owe him $180, but I have $465. So after I pay off the $180 that I owe, I have $285 left over."

575

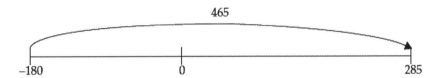

465

−180　　　　　　　　0　　　　　　　　285

Terra started her number line at negative 465 and drew an arching line that went 180 to the right, to negative 285. When I asked her to explain how this matched the context, she could not. She did not seem to be concerned that her answer ended up being negative 285 instead of positive 285.

After a couple of students shared their negative number strategies, a number of other meth- 580 ods surfaced. Ivan said that he subtracted a negative 180 to get the answer. Other students disagreed with his method, but they had to use other models (such as the chip model) to convince everyone that Ivan's method would give an answer of 465 + 180, not 465 – 180. The original context was not useful in making sense of this method or Ivan's confusion. 584

2

Making meaning for multiplication and division

As we move from addition and subtraction to multiplication and division, the questions that were posed in chapter 1 still apply, and we extend them to all four operations:

- When we see different number sentences that can model a single situation, what do we learn about relationships among operations?
- What does it mean to have a concept of addition, subtraction, multiplication, or division?
- What can we see about the operations through different representations (cubes, number lines, and so on)?

Furthermore, multiplication and division come with their own questions:

- What kinds of situations are modeled by multiplication and division?
- What issues must students work through in order to make sense of these operations?

• What ideas about addition and subtraction do students bring to their work with multiplication and division?

Ponder and take notes on these questions as you read through the following cases from kindergarten through grade 4. After reading the cases, review the questions again.

case 8

Bunnies and eggs

Bella
GRADE 1, SEPTEMBER

Because Easter was coming up, I decided to do some problems about bunny rabbits. After a discussion on the number of legs one bunny rabbit has, I drew a picture of a bunny on the board and asked the children to solve the following problem:

If one bunny has 4 legs, how many legs would 3 bunnies have?

I told them that they could use any manipulative they wished to solve the problem. I was quite interested in the various representations they came up with.

Jason built his rabbits from colored wooden blocks; each rabbit had a head, a body, and four legs. He came over to me and said, "Mrs. Waters, I got 12 legs." I asked him how he got the answer, and he told me he counted them. I asked him to draw me a picture of what he had done. Figure 2.1 shows his drawing.

Fig. 2.1. Jason's drawing of 3 rabbits, 4 legs each

Rashad used the large plastic keys we keep in a bucket in the room. He placed one key horizontally for each body, four keys perpendicular to it for the legs, and made three of these arrangements (fig. 2.2).

Fig. 2.2. Rashad's arrangement of keys representing 3 rabbits

I asked, "How many legs did you get?" and Rashad told me 12. When I asked him to show me how he got 12, he counted, pointing to each "leg" in turn. I was surprised that he didn't get confused about which keys were legs and which represented the body.

20

Carlita also used keys to represent the problem. First she made one row of four keys and told me that she had one rabbit. I asked her where the other rabbits were, and she said she would make them. I watched her build a second row of four keys, and then a third row (fig. 2.3).

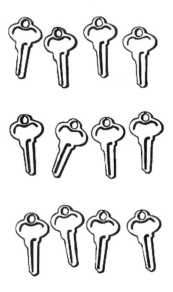

Fig. 2.3. Carlita's arrangement of keys, showing 4 legs for each of 3 rabbits

25

"See, I have 3 rabbits."

"How many legs are there in all?" I asked.

Carlita counted her keys: "12."

Kenya used interlocking cubes, snapping together three groups of orange and white cubes in an a-b-a-b pattern. She counted them all together to get her answer and made a picture of what she had done (fig. 2.4).

30

Fig. 2.4. Kenya's picture of cubes representing 3 four-legged rabbits

When I got to Flora, she had a row of 12 rocks in front of her (fig. 2.5).

35

Fig. 2.5. Flora's rocks, representing the 12 legs on 3 rabbits

"How many legs did you get?"

"I got 12."

"Can you tell me how you did it?"

"I counted one bunny first; then I counted the next bunny's; then I counted the next bunny."   40

"So how did you know how many legs there were in all?"

"I counted all of them."

Mark, Quincy, and Jerome were busy building their rabbits out of Legos. They built great looking rabbits with four legs, but time ran out before they could solve the problem.

The children were all so engaged in solving the problem that, even when I announced   45
lunchtime, they didn't want to leave. There was no one in the group who was not working on the problem.

The children enjoyed being given the problem to solve, though I was aware that some of them still have difficulty counting even those small numbers. Besides the children whose representations I have described here, there were some who were not able to figure out the total.   50

Several days later, I decided to give a similar problem with Easter baskets; this time I wanted to see what was going on with the children who had difficulty with the bunny problem.

I made 3 Easter baskets for my friends. In each basket, I put 3 eggs. How many eggs were there in all?

Again, I told the children they could use whatever manipulatives they might choose.   55

Jenna used the interlocking cubes. First she made a unit of 3 cubes and brought them over to show me. I asked her what she had, and she said that she had 1 basket.

"Where are the other baskets?" I asked.

"I haven't made them yet," she said, heading back to the table. Soon she was back again, this time with 2 units of 3 cubes.   60

"How many baskets do you have now?"

"2."

"How many baskets did I say were needed?"

"3."

"Where are they?"   65

Jenna went off again and returned with the third unit of 3. "How many eggs do you have?" I asked.

"I don't know. I haven't counted them yet." She proceeded to count all the cubes and soon arrived at her answer of 9 eggs.

Jenna really surprised me with her understanding of the problem. She very rarely partic-   70
ipates in an activity in a way that helps me understand what she really knows. Today I was impressed.

Junior also worked with interlocking cubes. He had 3 orange ones, 3 white, and 3 yellow.

"What do you have?" I asked.

"3 baskets."   75

"How many eggs are in each basket?"

"3."

"How many eggs do you have in all?"

"3."

Junior showed me how he counted: Each unit of 3 was "one" to him. I took one unit and   80
broke it apart. He counted them, "1, 2, 3," and agreed that they represented 3 eggs. I put them back together with the other two units of 3 and asked him how many eggs were there. Again he said, "3." I tried several ways to help him see that I wanted him to count the individual cubes, but it didn't help. He was unable to see the difference or sameness between cubes once they became a single unit of 3.   85

Several of the children had no difficulty with this problem, so for them I posed the following extension:

>   If I added 1 more egg to each basket, how many eggs would there be?

When I gave the second problem to Mark and Quincy, they both went away and soon returned with an answer. Mark explained, "I put 3 more on the 3 baskets. One more egg to 3   90
baskets, and that makes 12." Quincy had the same answer, but when I asked him how he got it, he said, "Mark told me."

Jason presented me with 3 groups of 3 interlocking cubes to demonstrate his answer of 9 to the first problem. When I asked him to solve the second problem, he added only a single cube and said there were 10. I repeated the question at least twice to see if he could figure out what   95
was wrong with his answer and how he could fix it, but he did not change his answer.

Rashad had no problem figuring out the first problem, using an arrangement of 3 rows of 3 keys each. When I gave him the second problem, he added 1 key to each group and said there were 12 eggs. Seeing how easily he arrived at the answer, I decided to challenge him with another extension: 100

> I have another friend, and I would also like to give this friend an Easter basket
> with the same number of eggs. How many eggs would there be in all?

"I added 1 more basket," he said. "4 baskets with 4 eggs: 16." Only after he gave an answer did he count the added keys. "See, I was right!" Rashad, it seems, has an ability to think about numbers at a level beyond his age.   105

As usual, I was unable to get around to all the children, but I learned more about what my class knows and how they handle problems. A couple of years ago, I wouldn't have attempted any of this kind of mathematics with children of this age. I would have thought that this is too difficult for them. How wrong I would have been!   109

case 9

Buildings, floors, and rooms

Annalisa
GRADE 2, JANUARY

I told the students that we would be making buildings out of cubes. (The activity comes from   110
Patterns, Teams, and Other Groups, a second-grade unit from *Investigations in Number, Data,
and Space,* 3rd edition [Pearson 2016].) Each cube was a room in a building, and we'd think
about the number of rooms on each floor and how many rooms in the whole building. "There's
one rule for our buildings," I said. "Each floor must have the same number of rooms and fit
exactly over the room below it."   115

As the students watched, I built a building that had one floor and two rooms. Then I added
cubes to make a three-floor building with two rooms on each floor. We imagined families of
tiny people living on each floor and agreed that each floor had a bedroom and a kitchen.

Once the context and the words "building," "floor," and "room" had been introduced, I
asked a series of questions about the building.   120

- How many rooms are on each floor of this building?
- How many floors does the building have?
- How many rooms are there altogether?

These three questions would be central to our discussions throughout this work.

I asked everyone to think about what would happen if I made the building higher. How   125
many rooms would there be in the building if it had 5 floors?

Caroline: If there were 5 floors, we would double 5—5 kitchens and 5 bedrooms.

Roger: I know that there's a kitchen and a bedroom on each floor. If you do 5 floors, I
would count by twos—2, 4, 6, 8, 10.

A show of hands indicated that everyone was on board with Caroline and Roger's thinking. I   130
moved on to ask about 8 floors. I asked the class to turn to a partner and talk about how they
would figure that out. When we came back together, Leighanne went first.

Leighanne: There would be 8 bedrooms and 8 kitchens—16 rooms.
About half the hands went up when I asked who shared Leighanne's idea.

Roger: I would count by twos again, starting from 5, because that was our last number.   135

I stopped Roger before he went any further to make sure that his classmates were focused on
what numbers he was referring to in our building.

Teacher: Are you talking about what we already know: there are 10 rooms on 5 floors?

Roger:	Yeah.
Teacher	So as everyone listens to Roger's idea, you need to keep that in mind. He's remembering that when we had 5 floors, we had 10 rooms.
Roger:	I just have to add 3 more.
Teacher:	You have to add 3 more what?
Roger:	3 more twos.
Teacher:	Why does Roger have to add on 3 more twos?
Luke:	He has 5; 6, 7, 8 counting by twos.

I placed our cube building in the center of our circle. It now had 5 floors with 2 rooms on each floor. I asked Luke to continue.

Luke:	What Roger means by 3 more twos, he starts with 5 floors. Then there would be 6, 7, and 8 floors—3 more stacks of 2.
Teacher:	Three more floors of 2 rooms.

I added 3 more two-room floors to the building and looked around the class. Then I followed up with a new problem. "Suppose I built it with 10 floors. How many rooms would there be?"

Jack:	You would just double it.
Teacher:	Double what? What's the "it"?
Jack:	Double the 10.

I wasn't sure if Jack was doubling 10—10 bedrooms or 10 kitchens—the way Leighanne had doubled the 8 floors, or if he was doubling the five-floor building—5 floors has 10 rooms so twice as many floors has twice as many rooms. As I asked Jack for more details, he became quiet. He may have lost track of what he meant, or perhaps, he had just lost track of the words. I checked in with the class.

Teacher:	If we double the number of floors, what will happen to the 10 rooms? Jack has given us all something to think about. This isn't just his question. How do we figure out how many rooms? How does the idea of doubling the building help us? How many rooms are in the whole building when we have 5 floors?
Thomas:	10.
Teacher:	When we double the building and we put on 5 more floors, how many more rooms will we be adding on to the building?
Thomas:	5.
Teacher:	Do you mean 5 floors or 5 rooms?
Thomas:	5 rooms.

It seemed that Thomas was having a difficult time visualizing and keeping track of the rooms and floors. I thought it would help if he held the model.

Teacher: Could you take the cube model and show us where the 5 rooms would be?   175

Thomas pointed to the top of the building and said, "Right here."

Teacher: If we add 1 more floor, how many rooms will we add?

Thomas: 1.

Teacher: How many rooms are on the first floor?

Thomas: 2.   180

Teacher: How many on the second floor?

Thomas: 2.

Teacher: How many rooms are on the fifth floor?

Thomas: 5. I mean 2.

Teacher: Every time we add a floor, we had how many rooms?   185

Thomas: 2.

Teacher: So if we add 1 more floor and we have 6 floors, how many rooms will we add on to the building?

Thomas hesitated.

Teacher: There's a lot to keep track of here. You have to keep track of how many floors   190
there are, how many rooms there are on each floor, and how many rooms there
are in the whole building, altogether.

In fact, this is precisely what makes understanding multiplication challenging for many second graders—they have to keep track of different units and how they are related. It's a lot for a young mind to juggle.   195

I decided it was time for the students to move on to work on their own buildings with 3 rooms on each floor. There would be other opportunities to pursue the idea of doubling the whole building. We worked together to build the first two floors of 3 rooms each, and once I was sure that everyone knew how to continue building more floors, I had them continue the activity in pairs.   200

The sample of student work below shows three different approaches to solving the problem of the number of rooms in a building with 10 floors, 3 rooms on each floor.

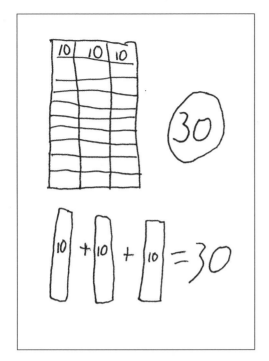

Fig. 2.6 Student A's work

205

Fig. 2.7 Student B's work

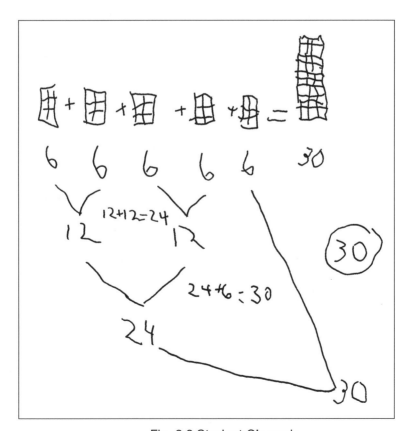

Fig. 2.8 Student C's work

case 10

Candy canes in packages

Janine
GRADE 4, DECEMBER

I sat with three girls today as they tried to tackle the following problem:

> There are 609 students at the school. How much would it cost to buy each one
> a candy cane? Candy canes are sold in packages of 6 for $ .29.   210

I have been trying to make the rounds and sit with a different group each day. It's interesting to see who has the concepts, who sits back, who leads the discussion, who is totally lost, which ones listen to each other, and which ones hear only their own voice.

The threesome that I sat with today is a new grouping. They have never worked together before, but they seemed to click on this problem.   215

Each started out working on her own for a few minutes; then they began talking. Almost immediately the three decided that the problem had something to do with the 6 times table—and that they had to go pretty far up the table to get to where they wanted to be. They started "6, 12, 18, 24, 30," and soon realized that there had to be a faster way.

Letitia, who grasps concepts pretty quickly, suggested that they should do 90×6 because   220 she had figured out it would be 540. Wow! Good for her, I thought. We have been working on multiplying numbers by multiples of 10, so I guess it clicked for her that if $6 \times 9 = 54$, so 6×90 would equal 540. I was hoping she would take it one step further and see that 6×100 would be 600, but she stopped there and neither of the other two saw this either. Maybe this was because when studying the 6 times table in third grade, they only went up to 6×9.   225

From 540 they decided that they had to add up by 6s to get to 609. This is where keeping track of their numbers became very difficult. Letitia, after some thought, said that $540 + 10$ more would equal 600. One of the others said that $540 + 10$ is equal to 550 and not 600. Letitia struggled to explain. She had the idea that 10 groups of 6 would get her to 600, but she kept confusing 10 and 10 groups of 6. I could see her struggling to keep track of her thoughts; I   230 could see her getting it and then having it fly out of her mind. She knew that 10 was important, but couldn't hold onto the idea that it wasn't 10 ones but 10 groups of 6 she was thinking about.

To help her out a little, I asked how many more she needed to get to 600 from 540. She answered 60. "Oh yeah—60 is 10 groups of 6!" She would grasp this idea for a while and then lose it again. She was really trying hard to hold onto the meaning of this 10!   235

So now they had 90 packages plus 10 packages for a total of 600 candy canes. They knew they needed 9 more candy canes. One more package would bring them to 606, but they still needed 3 more. Could they buy 3 separately? No, they came in boxes of 6. If they bought another box, they would have 3 extra. What would they do with them? Natalia said, "Let's just eat   240
them! We did the shopping. We deserve a prize!" All happily agreed that they would eat the 3 extras themselves.

Finally the group established that they had to buy 90 + 10 + 2 packages of candy canes. Because they didn't know how to multiply 102 × $.29, they decided to do it with the calculator. Their answer came out 2958, which they reasoned would be $29.58.   245

case 11

How do kids think about division?

Georgia
GRADES 3 AND 4, OCTOBER

I decided to begin this year by focusing on the four operations. I wanted to investigate my students' ideas more closely.

As I discussed my plan with a colleague and said I was particularly interested in learning how my eight-, nine-, and ten-year-old students thought about division, she was horrified. She believes that children need to be taught the operations in a certain order. In her mind, first comes addition, then multiplication, then subtraction, and then division.

My initial idea was just to expose kids to division problems early in their experience with numbers so that the process would be familiar when they came to the numbers that themselves implied division—decimals and fractions. But through my classroom research, I'm learning much more about how kids think about division, what they call division, and how they define division. Much of this learning comes from my observations of their written work.

Each week I have given the students story problems that I considered to be division problems, problems I would solve by using division. Here are some examples and a few of the kids' responses to them.

> Jesse has 24 shirts. If he puts 8 of them in each drawer, how many drawers does he use?

Vanessa wrote $24 - 8 = 16$, $16 - 8 = 8$, $8 - 8 = 0$, and then wrote 3 for the answer.

> If Jeremy needs to buy 36 cans of seltzer for his family and they come in packs of 6, how many packs should he buy?

This time Vanessa wrote $6 + 6 = 12$, $12 + 12 = 24$, $24 + 6 = 30$, $30 + 6 = 36$. I still need to ask her how many packs that gives her. But what made her add this time and subtract last time?

Other students use these same methods. Is it significant that sometimes they add and sometimes they subtract? What are their choices based on? I thought the problems about Jesse's shirts and the six-packs of seltzer water were the same kind of problem, and yet students treated them differently. On reflection, I wonder if the total number (24 or 36 in these cases) affects how kids approach a problem. If the total number is a familiar one, do they subtract (until they get zero), and if the number is less familiar, do they add, building up to the number, as Vanessa did for the second problem? Or do the contexts seem different to the children?

> Joni wants to build some bookshelves for her friends and family. If she bought 36 boards and she needs 4 boards for each bookshelf, how many bookshelves is she going to make?

Cory had clearly tried approaching this problem in more than one way. His paper was filled with tally marks, which seemed to be one approach he was thinking about it, while above the problem he had written 2 ÷ 36 = 28 ÷ 2 = 14. I decided to ask him about his thinking. I assumed he meant 36 ÷ 2 = 28, but I wasn't sure how he got the 28. I wanted to find out how he was really thinking about the problem instead of making assumptions.

Cory told me, "I thought it was times." Then he reread the problem aloud. "See, that's why I changed it to divided by. If it was 4 divided by, I would probably use 2 first so it would be easier. First I would do 2 divided by 36, and that equals 28, and 2 divided by 28 equals 14, so that's how I came up with 14. Because I knew divided by is half of whatever the number is, like 2 divided by 100 is 50."

I asked Cory, "Does that mean that 28 is half of 36?"

"Yes," he said, "because I know half of 30 is . . . wait a second . . . no, that isn't right. It would be 15 plus another 3, that's probably 18 and divided by that, which is 9."

Cory knew that 36 is made up of 30 and 6, and half of 30 is 15, and half of 6 is 3. Then he knew that 15 plus 3 is 18. He understands division in terms of halving, as he clearly states, "Divided by is half of whatever the number is." Halving is also implicit in his comment, "That's probably 18 and divided by that, which is 9"; he doesn't even have to say he halved it. And he knows that dividing by 4 is like halving twice. What about division that isn't based on half? Would that be division to him? What will happen when he has to divide by 3?

> You go into a pet store that sells mice. There are 48 mouse legs. How many mice are there?

Matthew organized his work beautifully. He wrote a key (m = mice, l = legs) and put his numbers in columns.

1 m	4 l
2 m	8 l
3 m	12 l
4 m	16 l
5 m	20 l
6 m	24 l
7 m	28 l
8 m	32 l
9 m	36 l
10 m	40 l
11 m	44 l
12 m	48 l

Then in a neat box he wrote, "12 *m* × 4 *l* = 48 *l*." Above the box he wrote the number 12. What does this say about Matthew's understanding of division? He knows that 12 is the answer, but he feels satisfied with a multiplication number sentence in which the answer is part of the problem rather than the answer to the problem. He knows how to find the answer, but instead of the number sentence I had expected, 48 ÷ 4 = 12, he wrote a multiplication number sentence.

During a conversation with classmates about a similar problem, Matthew said, "This is another division problem. It's 63 divided by 9. What number times 9 equals 63?—7." When I asked him to explain what there was about the problem that made it a division problem, he said, "I don't know, but it is. But my thinking is multiplication."

What does this say about kids' understanding of division if they use all the operations except division? As I look at how kids think about division, and how I had initially hoped that the work would help kids with fractions, I wonder in what way the two topics are connected. Do kids bump up against the same ideas in both division and fraction work? What does this say about how kids think about wholes and parts?

case 12

Are these kids or seeds?

Melinda
GRADE 2, NOVEMBER

On Halloween I had my second graders work on this word problem:

> There are 6 children sharing 45 roasted pumpkin seeds. They want to share them as evenly as possible. How many will they each get? 320

First I have to say that I was really amazed and impressed with the industry and confidence with which the children approached the problem. Almost everyone got right to work and seemed to be engaged. Here are some things that seemed interesting to me.

Maria, Nikita, and Su-Yin worked together. They each got 45 interlocking cubes and snapped them together in a row. Su-Yin's initial strategy involved taking one cube off her 325 collection of 45 so that she would have an even number left. When I asked her why she wanted an even number, she said so she could divide it in half. I asked her why she wanted to divide it in half, and what she planned to do next. She said she didn't know. I wondered whether she had some idea that she might be able to split her two even groups into three groups each somehow. On the other hand, maybe dividing something fairly made her think of halves and even num- 330 bers, without having any specific thought about needing six groups.

I never did find out because Nikita and Maria had a different strategy, which Su-Yin adopted. Maria started making 6 piles of cubes, first breaking off a stick of 5 cubes for each. She then gave each pile 2 more, and had 3 cubes left.

I left these three girls for a while and worked with other children. When I returned to them, 335 Maria was working by herself, drawing her 6 piles of 7 cubes, and Nikita and Su-Yin were arguing. Nikita was saying that each child got 7 seeds, and Su-Yin was saying each got 6 and Nikita was counting a kid as a seed. Su-Yin indicated her 6 piles of cubes and asked me, "Are these kids or seeds?" I asked her what she meant, and she said that Nikita thought that they were all seeds, but that she had made each of her groups by putting a cube to be a kid in the 340 center and then putting seeds around it. Therefore, her groups were 6 seeds and 1 kid each.

I was interested in Su-Yin's plan for representing and solving the problem, and I wondered what she had thought about in the process. I asked her to explain and show me exactly what she had done and thought from the beginning. She said she got 45 cubes, then put the 45 cubes in a big pile and made sure there were 45. I asked her why she had to have 45, and she said, "That's 345 how many seeds there are." She explained then that she wanted to make groups by putting a kid in the middle and putting seeds around it, so she started to take cubes from the 45, and then said, "Oh! I need to get 6 more cubes!" I asked her why, and she said, "Because those are seeds!"

My question: "Is this about keeping track of units again?" Su-Yin had to keep track of the numbers 45 and 6 from the start of this problem, and eventually there were some 7s and a 3. She had to think not just of the numbers and how they relate to each other but also what they represent in this problem. I think that her plan to represent a child and then give the child a fair share of cubes representing seeds was a good one.

But was it too much for her to hold onto at once? First she didn't realize that she couldn't take any of the 45 cubes to make children because those 45 represented the whole collection of seeds. Then, in her representation, she thought each group of 7 cubes showed a child and his or her seeds, still not realizing that "children" couldn't be taken from the "seeds" and that all the cubes had to be counted as seeds in the end. It was a lot to hold onto!

I am also intrigued by the fact that Nikita and Su-Yin were so clear about what they were disagreeing about. Su-Yin's statement that Nikita was turning a kid into a seed showed some clarity about what was going on and where the confusion was, even though it was in fact she who had turned a seed into a kid. I also wonder why Nikita was so sure she was right about the problem, the solution, and her representation of them, but could not convince Su-Yin.

Meanwhile, Derrick and William were having an interesting time with the problem. William, who is fairly able but not very confident, said immediately, "I have an idea!" His idea, which he shared with Derrick, was to start with 45 and keep taking off 6s. They did not want to use manipulatives or draw pictures. They did use William's plan, and subtracted 6 repeatedly from 45 "in their heads." They ended up with a list of numbers, run together and hard to read:

$$4\ 5\ 39\ 3\ 3\ 2\ 7\ 2\ 11\ 5\ 9\ 3$$

William did say that he took out 6s because that was 1 seed for each child. I wasn't sure whether their list of numbers told him how many seeds each child ended up with, but my colleague Lydia was in the room, and she had a conversation with him about it. She later explained to me that he started to divide their list of numbers in a way to show that each time he subtracted 6, he was giving each child 1 seed. However, he made mistakes about where to divide the run-together numerals, and ended up with 6 groups. It didn't bother him that the numbers he created by dividing up his string did not make sense in the context of the problem.

$$\overset{1}{}\ \overset{2}{}\ \overset{3}{}\ \overset{4}{}\ \overset{5}{}\ \overset{6}{}$$
$$4\ 5\ 39 \mid 3\ 3 \mid 2\ \ 7 \mid 2\ 11 \mid 5\ 9 \mid 3$$

When I joined William and Derrick, they had their list of numbers and had drawn 6 little bowls with 6 little seeds in each. I asked them what the bowls were and how many seeds they had in their picture. William replied that the bowls were the seeds for each kid. Derrick figured out how many seeds they had drawn by adding 6s, and said there were 36. William agreed.

Neither boy seemed bothered by the fact that they had accounted for only 36 seeds when there were 45 in the problem.

385

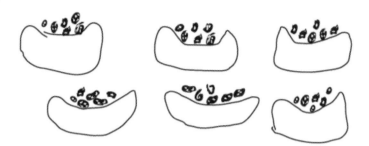

I asked them, "How many seeds would be left then?" They figured out that there would be 9 by counting on from 36 up to 45. When I asked what they could *do* with the extra 9 seeds, they disagreed. William suggested that each child could have one more seed, but Derrick said, "No, there's only enough for one kid. You would need another kid." I asked why, and he said because there was only "one more 6." He decided that maybe one of the existing kids could get 6 more 390 seeds, or 12 total, and that 3 could be thrown out. For some reason, he was unwilling to divide up a group of 6 seeds in order to give each child one more.

Apparently Derrick convinced William to give one person 12 and everyone else 6 (perhaps because I joked that maybe one of the kids was bossy or bigger or hungrier). When William explained his thinking to the class (I had him put out cubes to show his bowls of seeds), he had 395 a group of 12 and 5 groups of 6. He went back and forth between labeling his groups of 6 as one seed for each kid and as a single kid's share of seeds. I think he was confused because he initially took out groups of 6 and planned to give one seed in the group to each kid and do this as many times as possible, but then he began to see those original piles of 6 as the seeds for each kid. I wondered why he didn't distribute 6 of the remaining 9 seeds in the end. Why did he stop 400 distributing seeds when each of the 6 kids had 6?

Again, I have questions about how children can keep the "whole" group of seeds in mind while they think of particular ways to divide it into parts. There are many issues for children to sort out:

As they start dividing up the whole, what do their groups mean? 405

Are they collections for each child?

One seed for each child?

Are the children themselves represented in their diagram or model of the problem?

Although there was much confusion while these second graders worked on the problem, I have to say that they were remarkably able to make sense of a very complex question. 410

When dividing doesn't come out evenly

The action of sharing provides a context in which children can learn about the meaning of division. It also allows them to sort out some of the complexities of dividing whole numbers:

- What happens when the numbers don't divide evenly?
- Is it ever possible to divide a greater number into a lesser number?
- What sense could that possibly have?

In this chapter, we visit the same class twice as students explore what $5 \div 39$ might mean. In the spring of fourth grade, the students think about the question only in terms of whole numbers. What contexts are modeled by $5 \div 39$, and what would be the result of dividing 5 by 39? When they return to the question several months later as fifth graders, they are ready to consider their answer in terms of fractions. But their explorations now raise a new set of fascinating questions. As you read about these students' discussions, what ideas about division are underlined for you?

What new ideas must students entertain as they extend their work to the realm of fractions? And what ideas are you left to work through for yourself?

Next, we turn to a first-grade class that has been challenged with the problem of sharing 7 brownies among 4 people. As you read about the thinking of these young children, what other ideas about fractions are highlighted?

Finally, we read about seventh graders who use their understanding of whole number division to make sense of dividing into zero and dividing by zero. As you read about the thinking of these middle school students, what other ideas about division are spotlighted?

After reading the cases, review this introduction and take notes on your thoughts.

case 13

Can you divide 39 into 5?

MaryAnn
GRADE 4, APRIL

This year I came to understand much more deeply what it means to engage my students in discussion of mathematical ideas. I have become convinced that attention to mathematical thinking will serve them much better than exclusively drilling on computational procedures. However, as the standardized test approaches, I am concerned. It matters to the lives of these children that they score well.

For this reason, I decided to dedicate several weeks to the kind of problems they would face on the test. I distributed the textbook I have used in the past and assigned pages of drill. The day we were working on the "Division with Remainders" page, however, I realized that once we entered the realm of mathematical reasoning, we would never be far away from it. The session went like this.

> **Teacher:** Leo, what is problem 9? [*It's such a simple problem that I am almost not listening to the response.*]
>
> **Leo:** 5 divided by 39.

The problem on the page reads 39 ÷ 5. Hoping that Leo will correct himself, I ask him to repeat his statement, but he sticks with the same response. I ask the class if they agree with Leo, and they all say yes. Is this important? Should I restate the problem correctly? Are the children simply being inattentive or does this indicate a deeper lack of understanding?

> **Teacher:** What would the answer to the problem 5 divided by 39 look like? [*All hands go up. I call on Keesha.*]
>
> **Keesha:** 7 remainder 4.
>
> **Teacher:** If the problem is 5 divided by 39, is 7 remainder 4 the answer?

The students all say that it is. I wait for a while; we all wait for a while. The fact that we haven't moved on forces the students to review their work. They're beginning to realize they can take a risk here and discuss foggy ideas.

> **T.C.:** The number will be like—I say zero. You can't divide 5 with a 39 'cause it's a higher number. You can't divide a number that's lower by one that's higher.

At this point, the rest of the group seems to be neither convinced nor unconvinced but rather restlessly disinterested. They seem uncomfortable with my sticking with the same problem when they are all so sure the answer is 7 remainder 4. I am uncomfortable, too, and I wonder what they are so "sure" of.

I have Clarence repeat what T.C. said, and he states it correctly. The other students all agree that he has verbalized the statement accurately, but no one seems to have a feeling for what it means, whether it works or doesn't work, or how it might translate in a context. I sense that they are thinking only about rules for numbers without making a connection to what the problem means.

35

Teacher:	Is it true that you can't divide a number by a greater number?
Alejandro:	Yes, that's true. 5 can't divide by 39. If you had 39 kids and 5 dollars, you can't do that in a fair way. You will give 1 dollar to 5 persons and the other people will be mad.

40

I'm glad that Alejandro has introduced a context for us to think about. I'm also glad to hear him use the word "fair" and hope that the others will be triggered to think of the "fair shares" we had been studying not so many weeks ago.

Deon:	He's right, because the answer will be something about zero 'cause there is no answer for a problem like that.

45

Well, the kids didn't pick up on fair shares. Now I wonder about Deon's idea that if there is no answer, then the answer is zero. Does zero make sense to him in the problem $5 \div 39$? Is zero the answer to the problem or does zero mean there are no answers? Is the distinction between the two clear to him or to the others?

Jackson:	You cannot do 5 divided by 39 because on a calculator it won't work out. It will come out to be a number in the minus. It will be …

50

Jackson's voice drops and then he stops. It seems that everyone is confused and few have any sense of the difference between $39 \div 5$ and $5 \div 39$. How could they have sat for days, apparently comfortably, doing whole pages of these traditional exercises? What has happened to all our thinking and discussing and the conclusions that we drew when we worked on fractions? What is their sense about the numbers here? I ask whether it might help to think of another context. Deon is tentative but offers one.

55

Deon:	Well, 5 people and 39 desks. … [*He's not sure how to go on.*]
Cynthia:	What T.C. said is true. If there were 39 principals and I had 5 pieces of candy to give them, then only 5 principals could have a piece. The other 34 would be mad at me and I would lose my job.

60

As I'm trying to sort out why Cynthia is subtracting, I'm also wondering about whether I should introduce another context. What if there were 39 principals and 5 pizzas? Would that context help them to think in terms of fractions? What if I made the problem simpler, such as 1 pizza and 4 kids? I suggest both examples, but the children don't pursue them.

65

Shannon:	5 divided by 39 really gets me confused. I can't see it in my mind.

Shannon goes to the board. I ask her to write 5 divided by 39, but she writes 39 ÷ 5. She just doesn't want to confront what seems so foreign to her. She keeps writing 39 ÷ 5 no matter how many times we rephrase the problem. She says that she doesn't want to stretch any more and asks to sit down. It's time to end the lesson.   70

Throughout today's class, many children just couldn't see that 39 ÷ 5 and 5 ÷ 39 model two different situations. Those who could see the difference decided that 5 could not be divided by 39 because there was no fair way to do it. I wasn't sure what to do. Is this something to follow up tomorrow, or should I continue with my agenda of preparing for the exam?   74

case 14

Can you divide 39 into 5?—revisited

MaryAnn
GRADE 5, NOVEMBER

75

This year I am in the fortunate position to have moved up a grade, together with my class. The children I had last year in fourth grade are with me again this year as fifth graders. I am very pleased. They are delightful children, a pleasure to be with two years in a row. At the beginning of the year, we had much less work to do to establish norms of being in class together; there was already a sense of community among us. The several children who were new needed a couple of weeks to catch on, but they had good models in their classmates. This is especially helpful since we have some difficult circumstances to work with. For example, my class of twenty-eight children is very unbalanced by gender: twenty-one boys and seven girls. If I had been meeting this group for the first time, we would have had to do a lot of work to make sure that the girls had a voice in the class. I still have to be careful, but in general the girls feel at ease, even though they are so much in the minority.

In math class, most of the kids already know what it means to have a mathematical discussion. And it's fascinating to me to have the opportunity to see how ideas develop from one year to the next.

In November we were working on division. We had just finished a few sessions in which we looked at remainders in different contexts and saw them expressed as decimals or fractions. We also considered contexts in which it made sense to round up or down to the next whole number. Now I wanted to explore an extension: situations in which there are more sharers than the number of items to be shared.

I asked the class to think about 3 kids sharing 2 candy bars. Just as the discussion began, Leo looked puzzled and recalled a conversation that we had last year. He claimed that the class reached the conclusion that we couldn't divide a larger number into a smaller number. As he presented the facts of last year's discussion, others began to nod. They were recalling the conversation and the contexts we used in our $5 \div 39$ controversy. Now they were looking at me accusingly. How could I be asking them to divide 2 candy bars among 3 kids if we already "knew" that we couldn't do it?

This situation made me wonder about the wisdom of leaving students in the middle of a misunderstanding. Would they have understood any more if last year I had told them that we can divide 39 into 5? Would they have been as invested in today's discussion? Were they now having an intuitive sense that we could do it? Although it was not my planned entry point into this new division idea—I had intended to work with easier numbers—we stuck with $5 \div 39$ because the class had an investment in it. I began by writing on the board $5 \div 39$ and $39 \div 5$.

Anthony: I think that 39 ÷ 5 will be 7 remainder 4, but I think that 5 ÷ 39 will make a decimal number.

I wonder if he is thinking of a number less than 1, and I wonder why he went to a decimal rather than a fraction. I was surprised because fractions "look" more like "less than 1" than decimals do—at least they do to me.

Jackson: I think that you will end up with a fraction of a number because, well, because, 5 and 39—you can't divide 5 by 39 equally. I think it's going to be a number below 0.

I think that Jackson is headed in the right direction, especially when he says "a fraction of a number"—am I just hoping that the number is 1?—although it won't be below 0.

I wonder aloud about the answer being a fraction, and then about the idea that it would be below 0. I believe that if I had stuck with my original 2 ÷ 3 problem in the candy-bar context, this might have been easier to visualize. But I don't know if the students would have been so invested; they have a sense of ownership over the problems involving 5 and 39.

Alejandro: I agree with Anthony but not with Jackson. We had some story problems where the answers were decimals but they were not below 0. I think we could say that 39 ÷ 5 could be a decimal number. [*He goes to the board and shows how he solved for a quotient of 7.8.*] I think that this is what Anthony means.

Anthony says this is not what he means, but that he doesn't feel ready yet to explain. Alejandro used decimals to solve 39 ÷ 5, but did not try 5 ÷ 39 and did not address the crucial point of using a decimal to name a number less than 1. I'm pretty sure that this is where Anthony's going, but I respect his decision to remain quiet for now.

Darrell: I think 39 can't go into 5. I mean, it can go into it, but it's going to be a fraction, it's got to be a fraction. A larger number into a smaller number—5 can go into 39, but there's a remainder. No, it's not a remainder; it's not a number.

I really don't get what Darrell is saying. Does he think that fractions or decimals are only remainders? Why does he think that it's "not a number"?

Greg: I agree with Anthony and with Jackson because 39 divided by 5, no, 5 divided by 39 …

Greg repeats the two problems four or five times. There's something that he's trying to sort out. However, the numbers removed from context clearly have little meaning for him.

Leo: 5 divided by 39 is going to be a smaller number. You have 39 people and 5 candies.

I stop to ask the class which one of the notations, 39 ÷ 5 or 5 ÷ 39, expresses Leo's story. I want to see if we are at least making a connection between the context and the correct notation. Most of the students didn't get that last year.

Mitchell chooses the correct notation and explains that the answer would be pieces of candy   145
bars. (YES!)

Mitchell:	So, if each kid was going to get equal shares, they would have to cut the 5 candy bars into little equal pieces.
Teacher:	Can you name those equal pieces?
Mitchell:	They might be candy bars. 150
Teacher:	Can you name the fraction that they might be?
Mitchell:	[*After a long pause*] They wouldn't be able to do it.

DARN! We stop now to take a class poll. How many people think that you can do the problem
5 ÷ 39? How many think no you can't? The results: yes, 13; no, 15.

After a pause, Leo says that he wants to change his no to a yes. He starts to explain that   155
you cut each bar into 7 equal pieces, and then asks if he can go to the board. He draws circles
to show the 39 people and then draws five rectangles for the 5 candy bars. He shows that
partitioning 2 candy bars into sevenths will yield 14 pieces and then, without making the lines,
indicates that partitioning 4 candy bars will produce 28 pieces. He pauses and sees then that the
fifth candy bar will give him a total of 35 pieces. He then draws in lines to show that he has cut   160
the last bar into 11 pieces. Now he's satisfied because he has a total of 39 pieces.

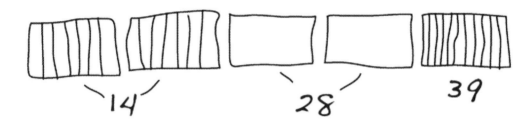

Cynthia quickly responds that this representation couldn't be correct because it isn't
equal shares. She seems sure of it. There are four rectangles with sevenths and only one with   165
elevenths. "That's a problem," she says.

As Cynthia talks, Tori goes to the board and points to the elevenths.

Tori:	Nobody would want one of these small pieces. There's something about Leo's solution that feels right, but something also seems wrong.
Maribel:	I think that Leo is on the right track because each person would only get a 170 really small piece, not anywhere like a whole candy bar. But Tori is right, too, because the shares that he drew aren't the same for each person.
Laila:	If I cut each of the 5 candy bars into 39 pieces and then give each kid 1 piece from each candy bar, you could have each kid have $5/39$ of a candy bar.

Laila wants to go to the board and draw hers. She draws 5 rectangles divided up into 39 equal   175
boxes. She is displaying some confidence and some clear mathematical thinking that I have not
seen before.

Anthony: I think the same thing, that each person will get 1 piece from the first candy
bar and 1 piece from the second and then from each one after that and will
end up with 5 little pieces, so $^5/_{39}$.   180

Alejandro: I was thinking that if you wanted you could take 5 from each candy bar over
and over again until you were done, but I think that I know that because of the
drawing Laila did.

Alejandro has learned something from the discussion; Laila's work made an impact on him. I'm
glad to hear him acknowledge her.   185

We ended the discussion right there, but continued a few days later. Since I happened to
have three visitors on that day (three colleagues from the professional development project I'm
in), I divided the class into four groups. Each group worked with an adult to come up with a
way to show $5 \div 39$. Time passed very quickly and we had little time for groups to report back
to the whole class.   190

Leo and Cynthia said that they didn't really have a name for their solution, but they were
ready to defend their thinking. Cynthia went to the board and drew a diagram that showed how
they divided 5 candy bars for 39 people.

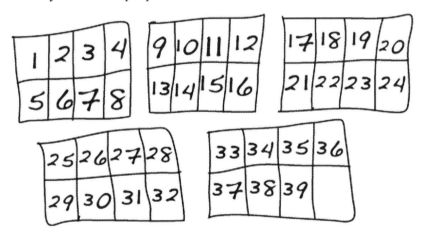

195

It was time to end class. Time was short and, even though all the groups had worked hard, I
think we were all feeling unsatisfied. Jackson looked at Cynthia's diagram and asked what
40 fortieths has to do with $5 \div 39$. I asked the students to think about that for their homework.

When we returned to the problem the next day, people were feeling refreshed again, ready
to take on Cynthia's diagram. While her drawing helped some of the students picture the prob-   200
lem, it raised even more questions:

• What is the last piece called? Is it $^1/_8$ or $^1/_{40}$?

• What's the whole?

• What happens if the last piece is divided into 39 pieces? What if it is divided into 40 pieces? 205

Do we know what $5/39$ means? Is "slightly more than $1/8$" a better answer than $5/39$ because it's clearer, even though it's less exact? What about $1/8$ and $1/39$ of $1/8$? What about $1/8$ and 1 of $1/39$ of $1/40$? When we say $1/8$, it's $1/8$ of what? When we say $1/40$, it's $1/40$ if what? If we cut the last piece into fortieths, each person gets $1/8$ plus $1/40$ of $1/8$. What happens to the extra fortieth? Do we keep on dividing it? (This is where we discussed the "piece," the "sliver," and the "crumb.") Some of 210 these questions I need to sort out for myself. 211

case 15

7 Brownies, 4 People

Lori
GRADE 1, NOVEMBER

I am participating in a seminar called "Making Meaning for Operations." As an assignment, we were asked to present to our students the following problem:

> I have 7 brownies and I want to share them among my 4 friends. How many   215
> brownies would each friend get?

At our next seminar meeting, we will share how our classes approached and solved the problem. It will be a very interesting conversation because our seminar includes teachers from prekindergarten through eighth grade. Following is an account of the response from my class.

My students have listened to, interpreted, and solved many story problems. However, this   220
problem was different from the combining and separating situations they were familiar with. This was a sharing situation.

I first attempted to do the activity as a whole class, but the students were baffled and I was besieged with questions. My responses were insufficient, and more questions followed. I felt that I could not attend to each student's questions as I usually do. I couldn't give my focused   225
attention to a single student when twenty others were approaching me at once.

So I decided to make 7 Brownies, 4 People a new center activity that students would circulate through, along with a few other math center activities already familiar to the class. This gave me the opportunity to have in-depth conversations with a few students at a time. Only then was I able to listen, to question, and to challenge each student's mathematical thinking.   230

Independently, many students came up with one of two different solutions: either they gave 1 brownie to each person and had 3 brownies left, or they gave 2 brownies to each person, giving 1 more brownie than was available. Two conversations captured the essence of the dilemma confronting my students. Although most students were unable to articulate it so clearly, it is interesting that some could.   235

Teacher:	Mathew, how many brownies did each person get?
Mathew:	I gave 8 brownies away.
Teacher:	Do you have 8 brownies to give away?
Mathew:	No.
Teacher:	No, then how many brownies do you have to give away? 240
Mathew:	7.
Teacher:	So, how many brownies would each person get?

Diane:	It is going to be hard, because 7 is not an equal number … because 7 is an odd number.	
Teacher:	So then what could we do?	245
Diane:	One kid has to get less than the others.	
Teacher:	Is there a way that each kid will get the same amount? Think about it. If you want, you could use these papers to represent the brownies.	
Mathew:	I know. I would have to split one up.	
Diane:	Oh, that's a good idea.	250
Mathew:	I would give them all 1 brownie, and then I would cut 1 in half.	

Mathew's solution was the most common response to my challenge. He first gave each person 1 brownie; then he gave another brownie to the first two people. He split the last brownie into 2 half pieces; the third and fourth people received only $1\frac{1}{2}$ brownies each.

Diane solved it differently. "I gave her 2, and him 2, and him 2, and the last person got a big one broken in half, which is like 2.

James did it still a different way. He understood that he needed to split the brownies into smaller pieces, but he didn't seem to have a strategy, at least not one he could explain. At first he split the brownies into different-size pieces. Then he started again. This time, he split each brownie into halves. He gave two halves to each person. Then, not knowing what to do next, he split 1 of the brownies into 4 pieces and gave 2 quarter-pieces each to the first and second person; then he gave the third and fourth people 1 each of the remaining 2 brownies. In the end, each person received 4 pieces, but two people received 4 half-brownies and the other two received 2 half-brownies and 2 quarter-pieces.

As students each grappled with the problem, they came to understand that the brownies   270
needed to be split. Once they had more pieces to share, they felt that their problem was solved.
The students split the brownies in such a way that each person received an equal number of
pieces, but not necessarily an equal amount of brownies.

By the time these students reach third grade, I expect that they will solve the problem
differently. That is, I would expect third graders to cut the brownies in a way that gives each   275
of the four people the same amount—$1^3/_4$ brownies. At first grade, I am simply pleased that my
students are willing to tackle the problem and have ways to interpret it that make sense to them.
Their study of fractions is still ahead of them.   278

case 16

Zero is special; zero is nothing

Jayson
GRADE 7, SEPTEMBER

Charlene and I have worked together for several years on district-wide math committees and   280
as district math specialists. Although Charlene has returned to her full-time math teaching at a
local junior high school and I am teaching mathematics education at a local university, we continue to work together on examining students' thinking about mathematics. Today, Charlene has
invited me to observe her students as they think about dividing a number by zero.

The class is a group of advanced seventh graders who have been identified as ready to take   285
a beginning algebra class a year or two ahead of most of their peers at the school. They have
been working on how rates of change, such as $3 per hour or 5 cookies per person, show up on
a graphical representation as the slope of a line; for example, for $3 per hour, the graph "rises"
vertically 3 units every time you move 1 unit to the right, or as the students would describe it,
the ratio $^{rise}/_{run}$ is $^3/_1$.   290

Charlene wants students to connect the previous images they have developed about fractions, ratio, and division to the new images they are developing about rates of change and slope.
As she has been thinking about how to help students interpret the ratio rise/run when the "rise"
is 0 or the "run" is 0, she has decided that she first needs to know how they think about fractions when either the numerator or denominator is 0. Do they know that when the numerator   295
is equal to 0, the fraction is equal to 0, but when the denominator is equal to 0, the fraction is
undefined? Do they know that when both the numerator and denominator are equal to 0, here,
too, the fraction is undefined? If not, what do they think about the meaning of such fractions?

Charlene and I devised five questions for students to answer individually to get at their
initial thinking about such fractions. They are to be prepared to explain their reasoning to their   300
peers, using pictures, diagrams, or stories to justify their answers. After recording their initial
ideas, the students will get together in groups to compare answers and try to reach consensus.
They will also need to decide how they will try convincing other members of the class that their
answers are correct.

Below are the five questions: 305

1. $^0/_7 = ?$
2. $^7/_0 = ?$
3. If $^x/_9 = 0$, then $x = ?$
4. If $^9/_x = 0$, then $x = ?$
5. If $x = 0$, then $^x/_x = ?$ 310

As the students went to work recording their answers and their ways of thinking about the problems, Charlene and I wandered around the classroom noting their initial responses. Most students had quickly written 0 as the answer to all five problems and were now going back to write a reason for each solution. I noticed that as some students thought more about the problems, they changed some of their answers. For example, although Tricia kept her answer of 0 for question 1, she changed question 2 to read $^7/_0 = 7$. To support her answers, Tricia wrote that the answer to question 1 was 0 because "you can't give 0 things to 7 people." She had drawn a picture of 7 people with nothing to distribute to them. For question 2 she wrote, "You can give 7 things to 0 people." She seemed to be trying to illustrate the action of distributing objects to people while focusing on the number of objects in her hand.

Brandon had also written 7 for the answer to question 2. To justify his answer he wrote, "It is right because if you divide 7 crayons by 0 people, you still have 7 crayons left." Both Brandon and Tricia seemed to be confused by the actions required by their interpretations of the division problems, and were left trying to decide what to do with the 7 leftover objects.

Other students had given non-zero answers to some of the other questions. For example, on question 5 Tyler had written $^3/_3 = 1$, $^2/_2 = 1$, $^1/_1 = 1$, $^0/_0 = 1$ and then added the words "zero can go into itself once." For question 4 Jessica wrote: "If $^9/_x = 0$, then $x = 10$" and her justification was that $^{10}/_{10} = 1$, so $^9/_{10} = 0$.

Most students, however, continued to believe that 0 was the answer to all five questions, although they supported their answers in a variety of ways. I noted later that their justification for question 2 often mirrored their response to question 1, as if they saw no difference between the two problems. Some of their initial reasoning about the questions included the following statements:

Ashley

Question 1: "Because if you split 0 up into 7 parts it is still 0."

Question 2: "Because it's just saying that there's 0 groups of 7 and that means there are not even any groups."

Cameron

Question 1: "There are no pieces of a 7 piece pie, nothing leaves 0."

Question 2: "You can't have 7 pieces of nothing."

Cameron added the following illustrations to support his written responses:

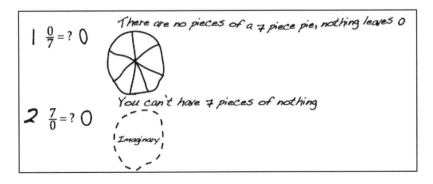

Ryan

Question 1: "If there are 0 cookies for 7 people, no one gets any cookies."

Question 2: "If there are 7 cookies and 0 people, no one gets any cookies."   345

Brindi

Question 1: "When you have 7 pieces of pie and there is nobody there, then nobody has pie."

Question 2: "No pie, nobody gets pie."

While Ryan, Brindi, and others had tried to think about division in terms of distributing cookies or pieces of pie to their friends, Mark and Adam were using other images of division to   350
support their answers.

Mark

Question 1: "$\frac{1}{7}$ is one seventh. $\frac{0}{7}$ is zero sevenths. If you have 0 of something, you have nothing."

Question 2: "7 zeros is nothing. $0 + 0 + 0 + 0 + 0 + 0 + 0 = 0$. You can't divide by 0."   355

Adam

Question 1: "There isn't a 7 in 0."

Question 2: "No 0 in 7."

Meanwhile, Kym had patiently written the same explanation on each answer, finally writing the statement with all capitals for emphasis, "ANYTHING MULTIPLIED OR DIVIDED   360
WITH 0 EQUALS 0!"

As students moved into groups to discuss the problems, one girl confidently announced to her group members, "Well the answer is always 0, isn't it?"

Charlene began working with Ryan, Brandon, Jacob, and Hayley. Hayley was sure that the answer to all five questions was 0, because she had "turned the problem around on all of   365
them—like on question 2, instead of 0 I did $0 \times 7 = 0$." The group was convinced that the second division problem, which they had recorded as $7/0 = 0$ could also be "turned around" and written as the multiplication problem $0 \times 7 = 0$.

Because no one in the group seemed to object to this interpretation, Charlene decided to point out a concern she had. "It looks like you turned the first division problem into multiplica-   370
tion differently than you did the second one. I agree that since $9/3 = 3$, I can write the related multiplication $3 \times 3 = 9$, but I'm not sure that is what you did on both of these problems. Why don't you look at that again?"

As Charlene moved on to another group, I stayed to observe what would happen. Hayley spoke as she wrote, "Oh yeah, the second one should be $0 \times 0 = 7$." It took awhile for the   375
implications of this last statement to sink in. "But that's impossible," Jacob said. At this point he picked up his calculator and entered $7 \div 0$ and pointed out the error message that appeared. "The problem doesn't make sense." Jacob crossed out the 0 he had written on his paper and wrote "impossible" instead.

As I wandered over to another group, I heard an argument over whether 7 cookies divided among 0 groups meant you had 7 cookies left, so $7/0 = 7$, or did it mean each person gets 0 cookies because there were no groups to give them to, so $7/0 = 0$. The voices arguing for "no groups, no cookies" seemed to be winning the debate, but before it could be resolved, Charlene was calling the class back together for sharing.

The class discussion quickly separated into two opposing sides, one side convinced that $7/0 = 0$, and the other side convinced that this division was impossible to do. Hayley and Jacob started the class discussion using their "related multiplication fact" argument that if $7/0 = 0$, then that would imply that $0 \times 0 = 7$. They also pointed out the error message on the calculator.

Cameron led the opposition camp. "We have all been told that 0 is a 'special' number," Cameron said, making quote marks in the air with his fingers to emphasize the word special. "Like 0 isn't positive or negative, and 0 isn't prime or not prime, and 0 isn't even or odd."

Benji objected to this last statement, saying that 0 was even, but Charlene wisely deferred that debate until another day.

Cameron continued, "Zero does special things. Like when you add with it, nothing changes, and when you multiply by it, you always get 0 instead of something else. Zero doesn't follow rules, and other strategies don't work for it. It has to be 0 because 0 groups of 7 is 0 and 7 groups of 0 is 0. It's a special number and we have to treat it differently."

Tyler looked very thoughtful as he countered Cameron's argument in favor of Hayley's. "If something is divided by 0 … then that can't equal anything." Tyler wrote $7 \div 0 = some\ answer$ on the board. Then he wrote $some\ answer \times 0 = 7$. "And," said Tyler, "no number works for $some\ answer$."

On the opposing side, Joey came to Cameron's support by focusing on the calculator issue. "Calculators have a problem with dividing by 0 because 0 isn't a number, and the calculator can't deal with nothing."

Cameron added to the calculator argument. "Calculators don't have a mind to work around abstract ideas like dividing by 0. The calculator can't divide by something that's not there."

Ashley also sided with Joey and Cameron: "I think 0 is a placeholder. It's something that people use to represent nothing." Ashley had been testing out questions 1 and 2 on her calculator. "When I go 0 divided by 7, I get 0, but when I go 7 divided by 0, I get error. It matters where you put the something and the nothing."

Renee turned the conversation back to Hayley and Tyler 's argument. "It's like fact families," she said, as she wrote the following on the board:

$$3 \times 4 = 12 \qquad 12 \div 4 = 3 \qquad 4 \times 3 = 12 \qquad 12 \div 3 = 4$$

"That's a fact family." Then she wrote the following:

$$0 \times 7 = 0 \qquad 0 \div 7 = 0 \qquad 7 \times 0 = 0 \qquad 0 \div 0 = 7$$

Renee concluded, "That last one's impossible."

Cameron countered, "Fact families are a theory that don't work for 0. Zero is special because everything else represents something and 0 represents nothing." Cameron produced his own "fact family":

$$0 \times 7 = 0 \qquad 0 \div 7 = 0 \qquad 7 \times 0 = 0 \qquad 7 \div 0 = 0$$

420

Jacob tried to get Cameron to see the implications of his previous argument: "It's impossible for 0×0 to equal something like 7, and that's what you're saying when you write $7 \div 0 = 0$."

Cameron replied, "No, I'm saying $7 \div 0$ doesn't equal anything, so it's 0."

At this point Charlene asked Cameron, "So are you saying that the problem $7 \div 0$ has no solution?" I saw what Charlene was getting at. I, too, wondered if Cameron was using zero to 425 indicate that there was no solution, since in Cameron's mind *zero is nothing.*

I slipped quietly out of the classroom as Charlene turned the conversation to slopes of lines where either the "rise" or "run" is zero. As I walked to my car, I wondered about the issues students had raised today through their comments about zero.

Does the belief that zero is "special" or that zero is "nothing" get in the way of seeing zero 430 as a number? Do their ideas about the role that numbers play in multiplication and division (e.g., number of groups, number of objects in each group) prevent students from making sense of division by zero? Do these students see division in two different ways, both as distributing objects to groups (partitive division) and measuring out groups of a certain size (measurement division)? What images might these two different interpretations provide? 435

I also wondered why their recent work with slopes and rates of change had not entered into the students' conversations. What new images of division by zero might come to mind as Charlene asks students to interpret slopes where the "rise" or the "run" is zero? What would have happened if these students had used images of rate, ratio, or slope to justify their thinking?

As a secondary math teacher, I know that each time we enlarge the number system—from 440 counting numbers, to integers, to fractions, and so forth—we have to renegotiate the meaning of addition, subtraction, multiplication, and division. That is, what images of operations still hold true, and what images need to be extended or modified? I had never considered, however, that this renegotiation of meaning of operations has to take place when we enlarge the number system from the set of counting (or natural) numbers to the set of whole numbers. What a 445 difference including zero as a *number* has on our understanding of operations. Do we ever give students an opportunity to make sense of zero as a number? Have I? 447

Greater than, less than, equal to

The first two chapters of this casebook showed that students first encounter number through counting and that they can develop initial meaning for the operations as they solve problems by counting. The third chapter showed that the operation of division, along with situations such as sharing, which are modeled by division, introduce a new kind of number, called fractions, that can fall between the counting numbers. There are many things to learn about fractions, including how they are written with two numbers to represent a single quantity.

A fraction is a quantity formed when 1 whole is partitioned into equal parts. The unit fraction $1/b$ is the quantity formed by 1 part when the whole is divided into b equal parts. The fraction a/b is the quantity formed by a parts of size $1/b$. For example, $1/4$ is the quantity formed by 1 part when the whole is divided into 4 equal parts. The fraction $3/4$ is the quantity formed by 3 parts of size $1/4$.

In this chapter, we encounter students who are working to understand how the two numbers that make up a fraction (the numerator and denominator) together determine the size of the fraction. Using diagrams and reasoning about what the numerator and denominator represent, the students determine which of two fractions is greater. We also find students who explain how two different fractions can actually be the same size, that is, how two fractions can be equivalent.

As you read the cases, take notes on the ways different students determine which of two fractions is greater, and how they know that two fractions are equivalent. Are any of these ideas new to you? What other ways do you have to compare fractions?

case 17

Which is greater? How do you know?

Faith
GRADE 4, MAY

Toward the end of our unit on fractions, my students placed fifty fractions on a number line. While they worked on this task, I told them to be aware of their thinking as they decided which of two fractions was greater so we could discuss their thinking later.

A few days after this activity, I wrote the following on chart paper to launch our discussion: 5
Which is greater, $1/2$ or $2/3$?

Harry: $2/3$ is greater because $1/2$ is only half, and $2/3$ is more than $1/2$. You can see it if you make two squares and split one in half and the other one in thirds.

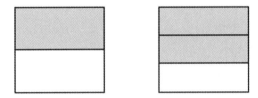

Teacher: What are you comparing in these two models? 10

Harry: The parts that are shaded. $2/3$ is greater than $1/2$.

Teacher: Any other ways of thinking about these two fractions?

Annie: In my mind, I see two circles, one split in thirds and the other in two halves. I compare the parts that are left, you know, the parts not shaded in. $1/3$ is smaller than $1/2$, so $2/3$ is greater than $1/2$. 15

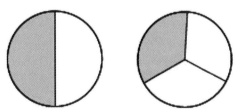

Teacher: Are there any other ways of thinking about these two fractions?

Chuck: I compare the fractions this way: When I see $1/2$, I know that 1, the numerator, is half of 2, the denominator. But half of the 3 in $2/3$ is $1\frac{1}{2}$ thirds, so I know that $2/3$ is greater. 20

I asked Chuck to come to the board to show us.

Chuck: Well, 1, the numerator, is half of 2, the denominator, so you can write just $\frac{1}{2}$. And one-half of the 3 in $\frac{2}{3}$ is $1\frac{1}{2}$. You could write $1\frac{1}{2}$ over 3 to show it. [*He writes this on the board.*] The $1\frac{1}{2}$ over 3 equals $\frac{1}{2}$, so you can see that $\frac{2}{3}$ is bigger than $\frac{1}{2}$, because $1\frac{1}{2}$ is smaller than the numerator, 2.   25

$$\frac{1\frac{1}{2}}{3}$$

As I looked around the room, I noticed a few students nodding in agreement with Chuck's explanation about the numerator being more than half the denominator. Others were just listening quietly. I decided to go on to another problem.

Teacher: Which is greater, $\frac{7}{8}$ or $\frac{3}{4}$?   30

Gary: That's easy; $\frac{7}{8}$ is greater because $\frac{1}{8}$ is less than $\frac{1}{4}$.

Teacher: Can you say more?

Gary: You need $\frac{1}{8}$ more to make $\frac{7}{8}$ a whole, and $\frac{1}{4}$ more to make $\frac{3}{4}$ a whole. Because $\frac{1}{8}$ is smaller than $\frac{1}{4}$, then $\frac{7}{8}$ is more.

Teacher: Do you have a picture in your head? What should I draw?   35

Gary: Draw two squares, and divide one in eighths and the other in fourths. Shade in 7 of the eighths and 3 of the fourths. When you compare the eighth to the fourth, you can see that $\frac{1}{8}$ is smaller so that means $\frac{7}{8}$ is more than $\frac{3}{4}$.

I drew the following picture according to Gary's directions:

40

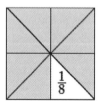 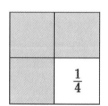

Teacher: Are there any other ways of thinking about these fractions?

Jesse: Well, $\frac{6}{8} = \frac{3}{4}$, and one more eighth is more, so $\frac{7}{8}$ is more.

Teacher: How do you know that $\frac{6}{8} = \frac{3}{4}$?

Jesse: Just look at the picture. You need to take away $\frac{1}{8}$ from the $\frac{1}{4}$ for it to equal $\frac{3}{4}$.   45

I now asked the class to think about generalizations of how to compare fractions.

Teacher: Can you talk about how you think about comparing any two fractions? Do you have a rule that helps you?

Ami:	Well, when there's a 1 on top in both numbers, then the smaller denominator is bigger.
Teacher:	Can you give me an example?
Ami:	Like ¹/₆ and ¹/₃. They both have 1 for numerators, but the smaller number, the 3, is a bigger piece.

50

I drew a picture to illustrate what Ami was saying.

55

Many students agreed with Ami's explanation.

Teacher:	Does this work all the time?
Many voices:	It always works when the numerator is 1.
Teacher:	How about when the numerator is greater than 1?
Rea:	When the numerator is more than 1, then the numerator has to be more than half the denominator to be bigger. Like ²/₈ and ³/₆; 3 is half of 6, but 2 isn't even close to 8. It would have to be a 4 to be half, so ³/₆ is more.
Teacher:	Would this work all the time? Can we try another example?
Ami:	Let's try ⁶/₈ and ⁴/₆.

60

She comes to the board and draws the following:

65

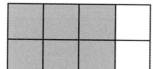 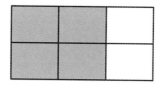

Ami:	This one is harder because both numerators are 2 away from the denominators. The half rule doesn't work here.
Jesse:	Yeah, but you can tell by looking at whatever's left over. The fraction that has the smaller part left is the greater fraction.
Teacher:	Hmm, can you say more?
Jesse:	If the white part on the ⁶/₈ is smaller than the white part on the ⁴/₆, then it means ⁶/₈ is greater.
Teacher:	You're comparing the unshaded parts. How much is not shaded in ⁶/₈ and ⁴/₆?
Jesse:	In ⁶/₈, there is ²/₈ not shaded, and for ⁴/₆, there is ²/₆ not covered. And ²/₈ is smaller than ²/₆, so ⁶/₈ is greater.

70

75

Ami:	Yeah, there is more covered on the $^6/_8$ than the $^4/_6$, so $^6/_8$ is greater.
Teacher:	So we've seen that the "half rule" doesn't apply to all pairs of fractions.

Previous to this episode, we had talked about comparing any two fractions with 1 as a numerator. Students knew that the fraction with the lesser denominator would be the greater 80 fraction because the piece would be larger. They explained, for example, that if a cake is shared among more people, the piece you get is smaller. Today it was interesting to hear students beginning to articulate other generalizations. For example, if both numerators are the same distance away from the denominators, the "unshaded" part is smaller when the denominator is greater—and that means that the fraction with the greater denominator is more. They also 85 specified how to compare any fraction to $^1/_2$. 86

case 18

Discovering common denominators

Nelly
GRADE 4, MARCH

Toward the end of our work on fractions, one of the assessment questions I gave to the class involved comparing $3/4$ and $5/6$. Are they the same size? If not, which is greater? I was puzzled to find that only four students answered the question correctly and gave an explanation that I considered adequate. Some students determined that $5/6$ was greater, but they drew diagrams that were inconclusive. Some students drew accurate pictures but didn't offer an explanation. Some students remembered a conjecture the class had come up with earlier—"the greater the denominator, the smaller the piece"—but misapplied it to this situation, concluding that $3/4$ must be greater. I decided the problem warranted further exploration by the class. 90

Several days later, I reminded the class about the problem and told them, "When I looked over your papers, I noticed that all of you agreed that $3/4$ is not equal to $5/6$, but you were thinking about this problem in many different ways. Also, even though you knew they were not the same amount, you do not agree about which one is more. I think we'll work on this some more today. I'm going to give you some graph paper and have you work together on this problem. I'm sure you will find a lot to talk about in your groups. Share your ideas and see if you can come to some agreement. The graph paper might help you draw your pictures more accurately. Lots of kids said that was a big problem for them." 100

I handed out the graph paper, and they got to work very eagerly. As they started, I interrupted briefly to ask, "When you're making your drawings, do the two 'cakes' need to be the same size?" Students nodded, and I asked several of them to restate that principle and suggest how they might make cakes that could be fourths and sixths and were the same size. Someone suggested using a 6-by-6 square, and that idea was adopted by many. 105

After students had worked for about twenty minutes drawing on their graph paper and sharing ideas, I invited them to make individual posters. Each poster should explain their ideas and be illustrated by graph-paper drawings. 110

The next day, we taped the completed posters to the board and gathered for a "mathematics convention." I introduced it by saying, "After your work together, I'm pretty sure that you all agree now that $5/6$ is more than $3/4$. What is your proof that this is true? Let's look at the posters and share ideas. Isn't it fascinating that we can all agree on an answer and still find it so interesting to talk about the different ways we have to prove it?" 115

Eli, who had worked so hard on his drawing earlier, delighted in his ability to produce a very accurate drawing with the graph paper. Using a 6-by-6 grid, he drew pictures to show the two fractions (fig. 4.1). Accompanying his drawing, Eli wrote, "$5/6$ is bigger than $3/4$ because it has more colored in." 120

Fig. 4.1. Eli's poster comparing the
two fractions

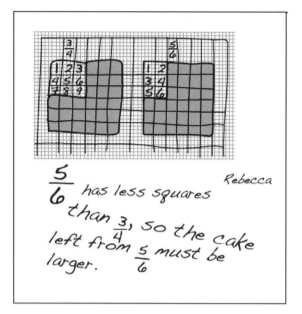

Fig. 4.2. Rebecca's poster comparing the
two fractions

Rebecca's poster is shown in figure 4.2. Rebecca explained that when she wrote, "5/6 has less squares than 3/4," she meant the numbered squares, those that were not included in the amount of cake represented by 5/6 and 3/4.

Matt's poster (fig. 4.3) illustrated the same principle Rebecca meant to show.

125

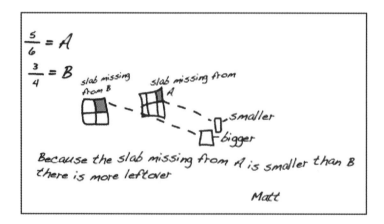

Fig. 4.3. Matt's poster comparing the two fractions

It was Bibiana's work, however, that caught the attention of the class and created the most discussion (fig. 4.4). Bibiana, in her characteristic way, had struggled with her picture until she had finally figured out a way, not just to show that $5/6$ was more, but also to show how much more it was. Like many other students, she had worked on a 6-by-6 grid, but as she worked, she began to see the portions as twelfths, not fourths or sixths. She had completed her poster by herself, although she had talked with her group mates and me about it. She ended up making two representations of the two fractions. The first representation showed the 36 individual squares, and in the second she had labeled the twelfths.

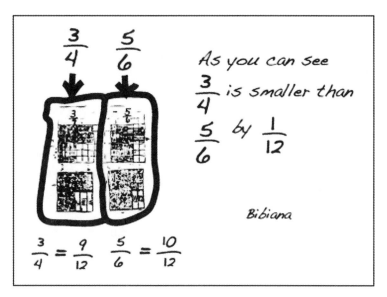

Fig. 4.4. Bibiana's poster comparing the two fractions

Many students seemed quite attentive to the conversation that resulted. Rebecca began, "I can see on your poster that the cakes are the same size. They need to be the same size."

Matt, using his own poster language of "slabs," chimed in. "Yeah, and I see you take out six or nine squares. You take out six squares from the $5/6$ and nine squares from the $3/4$. So it's like $5/6$ is A and $3/4$ is B. There is a slab missing from B and a slab missing from A; $1/6$ is less than $1/4$, so you're only taking $1/6$ from A but $1/4$ from B."

Max, one of the few students who had been able to explain the problem correctly and thoroughly the first day, still got tangled up in the language when he tried to explain it today. "When you shade in $3/4$ or $5/6$—the part that's not shaded—if it's bigger than the one that's colored in … oh, I can't say it!"

Jillian, who also had been successful the first day, tried to help. "You mean the piece that's not colored in from the $3/4$?" From here, the conversation moved quickly, and there seemed to be a number of students trying to find the words for what they were seeing pretty clearly in Bibiana's poster.

Matt tried again, this time using new language that matched Bibiana's representation instead of his own. "I see what you did. You translated the fourths and sixths into twelfths. Instead of having to compare fourths and sixths, they're both twelfths now. This is a very practical way. I like your way." 155

I asked, "What do you mean by 'practical,' Matt?"

Rebecca volunteered, "It's easy to understand, and it's simple. It's practical."

Jillian expanded on the idea: "You can really see it. There are $9/12$ in $3/4$ and $10/12$ in $5/6$."

Bibiana's poster and this conversation had been particularly satisfying. It seemed that all the students had had enough experience with the problem and a chance to draw careful pictures 160 with the graph paper so that Bibiana's discovery of common denominators made some sense to them.

However, as always seems to happen in a classroom, we were not allowed to rest content and free from confusion for long. Kalina presented the last poster, which included her own conjecture: "$5/6$ is greater than $3/4$ because 5 is more than 3 and 6 is more than 4." 165

As my students puzzled over her idea, I realized we still had a long way to go. Kalina, who usually understands math concepts and had shown particularly strong intuitive understanding of fractions, had drawn some representations in defense of her conjecture. It was as if she had grabbed at an idea that sounded good in words, drawn some pictures, and hoped she had proved something. 170

I realized I had some more pondering to do myself. I reminded myself that an understanding of these concepts develops slowly over time. Bibiana had given us a clear direction and a sense of satisfaction, but we still had struggles ahead. 173

case 19

Equivalent fractions

Malik
GRADE 5, APRIL

In one of our class discussions, we had found several fractions equivalent to $^1/_5$, including $^2/_{10}$, $^4/_{20}$, and $^8/_{40}$. I asked the students what they saw.

Many of the students said the numbers were doubling. We discussed whether or not the fractions, themselves, were doubling. Some of the students answered, yes, they were doubling the fractions.

In order to clarify some vocabulary, I talked about how the numerators and denominators were doubling. Whether the value of the fractions doubled, this was something we'd need to think through.

Macario said that he thought the fraction was still the same but looked different. In order to communicate his reasoning, he drew a diagram.

 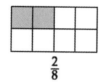

He pointed out, "When you double the numbers in the fraction, the fraction will still be the same."

Macario then related this idea to another case of equivalence we had recently discussed. He explained, "The answer to the fraction never changes, like when you add $5 + 2 = 7$ and $2 + 5 = 7$. The answer never changes, only the numbers."

Rabia said, "When you take a fraction and double the numerator and denominator, it gets smaller, because you split the pieces in half." But when pressed, she said that the fraction didn't get smaller, but the pieces were smaller.

Ida picked up on Rabia's idea and drew a picture to illustrate.

She showed that when the denominator increased from 3 to 6, the pieces got smaller. But if you take two of them, you have the same amount as $^1/_3$.

175

180

185

190

195

197

case 20

Today's number is 1

Zura
GRADE 4, MARCH

I asked seven students to join me in a small group with their papers showing their ideas for how to make 1 using only fractions (e.g., $3/4 + 1/4$, $1/2 + 1/2$). I wanted to see how these students were making sense of numbers like 4/4. I wondered if they would be able to talk about why, when the numerator and denominator were the same number, the number is always equal to 1.

Teacher:	I noticed that many of you were making equivalent fractions for this task.
	[*I wrote down the numbers suggested by the students.*]

$$8192/8192 \qquad 9186/9186 \qquad 4/4 \qquad 8/8 \qquad 16{,}224/16{,}224 \qquad 16/16$$

Teacher:	What patterns do you notice?
Iris:	I notice that the top and bottom numbers are the same.
Betsy:	You mean, the numerator and denominator.
Iris:	Yeah, that's what I mean.
Teacher:	Can someone tell me why this works? Why, when you have the same number for the numerator and the denominator, does it equal 1?
Betsy:	Oh, I know! 16 pieces are in the whole, and you have 16 pieces. That equals one whole.

The other students nodded and said they agreed with Betsy.

Teacher:	Will this always work? When you have the same number for the numerator and the denominator, will it always equal 1?
Kurt:	Not with negative numbers.
Iris:	Not with prime numbers or 13. You can't divide 13 in half.
Andy:	You don't have to divide 13 in half. You can have a fraction that equals $13/13$.
Iris:	Oh.
Teacher:	What were you thinking about, Iris? Why won't 13 work?
Iris:	I think it will work now. Wait, does the shape always have to be a rectangle or a square?
Teacher:	What do you mean by that?
Iris:	Can you come back to me?

I appreciated Iris's honesty and her willingness to take some time to listen and think about what she had just said.

Louis: It won't work on *all* numbers, but on all the numbers I tried, it worked. I kept doubling my numbers, and it worked.

Lili: It works all the time. If you break up a whole into an equal number of pieces, you can put them back together, as long as they are the same number of pieces—like puzzle pieces that you put back together. The denominator is like the number of pieces in the whole puzzle, and the numerator is the number of puzzle pieces in the fraction. 230

Betsy: It will always work if you have the numerator and denominator as the same number. It will always equal one whole, like 16 pieces in the whole square; $^{16}/_{16} = 1$. I think ... it's really hard to say in words. 235

Andy: It will always work. If you have 16 puzzle pieces and 16 spaces, it would always work. I'm having trouble saying what I mean. I understand it in my head. 240

Conor: Yeah, I could prove it to my brother, but not right now.

Lucas: I know what to say, but I can't remember ... what is a numerator and a denominator again?

We stopped to review the definitions of numerator and denominator, and then returned to the generalization on the table. 245

Lili: It will always work! I know it will always work! But maybe not with negative numbers, but most people don't work with negative numbers. Is there such a thing as negative fractions?

Lili looked around the table. No one had an answer for her, but everyone seemed to agree that this was a puzzling question. 250

I chose not to answer Lili's question, either. For now, I wanted students to work with images of fractions in terms of a whole unit divided into parts—parts they can count with whole numbers. If Lili felt solid with those ideas and was ready to think about negative fractions, she now had a question that would be useful for her to mull over.

As I review this discussion, I see that Iris has some misunderstanding to work through. I'll 255 need to give her more experiences that allow her to think about a variety of fractions, to help her see fractions of lengths (not just of shapes), and to place fractions on a number line. I'll also need to pay more attention to where Conor and Lucas are.

But from their comments, it seems that Lili, Betsy, and Andy were holding onto the meanings of numerator and denominator, together with an image of what fractions are. Lili's image 260 of a jigsaw puzzle—thinking of the number of pieces in the whole puzzle as the denominator and some number of those pieces as the numerator—helps to make the general claim. Lili states adamantly, "It will always work!"

But then Lili reconsiders. She seems to be aware that the puzzle image implies numerators and denominators greater than zero. She knows the puzzle doesn't help her think about fractions in which the numerator or denominator might take on negative values. 265

Although Lili doesn't mention it, the puzzle image does not help one think about $\frac{0}{0}$, either. In fact, that is the exception to the rule the students are considering. At some future time, they will learn that $\frac{a}{a} = 1$ for all values of a not equal to 0.

I am interested in Louis's comment that it won't work on all numbers, but on all the numbers he tried, it worked. He recognizes that it's not enough to test a general claim on specific cases to conclude that the claim is true over an infinite set. But if he returns to the meaning of the numerator and denominator, will he be able to see a general claim for the numbers we are considering here in fourth grade? That is, implicit in our work on fractions, denominators are always greater than or equal to 1; numerators are always greater than or equal to 0. And within these constraints, whenever the numerator and denominator are equal, the fraction is equal to 1. 270 275 276

case 21

Fraction flags

Kate
GRADE 2, MARCH

"Fraction Flags" is set of activities used in *Attributes of Shapes and Parts of a Whole*, the second-grade unit on Geometry and Fractions from *Investigations in Number, Data, and Space* (3rd ed., Pearson 2016).   In these activities, flags are used as a context for looking at both unit fractions ($\frac{1}{2}$, $\frac{1}{3}$, $\frac{1}{4}$) and non-unit fractions ($\frac{2}{3}$, $\frac{3}{4}$). 280

Prior to the lesson described here, the students had worked with unit fractions. They had colored in and labeled flags that were divided into two, three, or four parts, coloring each section of a flag a different color. For example, for a flag that was divided into thirds, a student might color one section red, one blue, and one green, and label them $\frac{1}{3}$ red, $\frac{1}{3}$ blue, and 285 $\frac{1}{3}$ green.

In this activity, the students use the same context to explore flags that have more than one part in the same color. We began by referring to a chart we had made that showed flags divided into different numbers of parts. For each flag, the chart showed the number of parts and what the parts were called in both words and numbers (e.g., half and $\frac{1}{2}$). 290

We reviewed what each unit fraction was called. Then I showed them the flag of Nigeria, which is divided into vertical thirds: the left and the right thirds are green, and the middle third is white.

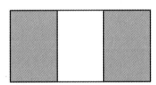

We talked through what each part is called. I explained that because two of the thirds are 295 green, we say that two-thirds are green, and we write it as $\frac{2}{3}$.

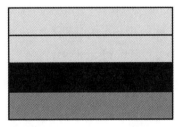

When we looked at the flag of Colombia, which is divided into horizontal quarters, the discussion quickly moved into the territory of equivalent fractions. The top half is yellow, the next quarter down is blue, and the bottom quarter is red. I asked who could tell me how many parts were in the flag. I called on Keegan.   300

Keegan:	Four.
Teacher:	There are 4 parts. How much of the flag is red? Colin?
Colin:	A quarter?
Teacher:	OK, one-quarter. [*I wrote: 1/4 is red.*] How much is blue? Holly? 305
Holly:	One-quarter.
Teacher:	[*writing*] One-quarter is blue. And how much of the flag is yellow? Sadie?
Sadie:	Two-quarters.
Teacher:	[*writing*] Two-quarters are yellow.
Joshua:	[*speaking with certainty*] That means a half. 310
Teacher:	That means a half? How do you know?
Joshua:	Because two-quarters have already gone by [*referring to the red and the blue having gone by in our discussion*], so another two-quarters would be another half. But if they are both yellow, then both yellow ones combined together would be a half. So since there are two yellow spots, it would be a half. 315

Reed looked eager to speak, so I asked if he wanted to add something.

Reed:	What he is trying to say is that two-quarters makes one half, because one-quarter is this big and another is this big, so that makes it a half. And two halves, because there are two over here [*points to the red and blue*] and then two over here [*points to the yellow*], and they're both the same. 320
Joshua:	But the bottom half is red and blue, so that makes both of them a quarter. But the top is all yellow, so that makes it a whole half.
Reed:	Because the top is kind of, since it's all one color, that makes it half is one color, and then a quarter is blue and a quarter is red. But if you put them together and pretend they were all blue or all red, it would show that the two bottom ones were a half and the top ones were a half. 325
Teacher:	So, can someone else say what Reed just said?
Keegan:	I think what Reed is saying is if there are two quarters out of four, it's basically half.
Teacher:	And do you remember why he said it was basically half? How he kind of proved it? 330

Keegan:	It's like the same length as each other. The bottom ones are just the same as this [*points to the yellow*], so it's half.
Reed:	It's more like a line of symmetry.
Teacher:	So come up and tell us which is the line of symmetry, Reed.
Reed:	Here's where it splits in half [*he points to the line between the yellow and blue sections*]. And this is the line of symmetry between the quarters [*points to the line between the red and blue sections*], and if you color over that, the line of symmetry is the line between the halves.
Teacher:	You're saying it's like there's a line here that makes it a quarter, and if you color over that line, then that line is invisible and then it's a half. And Tracy is shaking her head yes. You agree with him Tracy? [*She nods.*] Colin, you've been dying to talk. What did you want to say?
Colin:	Because it's like red is 25¢, blue is 50¢, one yellow is 75¢ and one more is a dollar.
Teacher:	You're thinking about it as money! That's really cool. If you're thinking about it as money, then this would be 25¢ [*points to a quarter of the flag*] and this would be 25¢ [*points to another quarter*]. This would be 75¢ [indicating three quarters of the flag], and this [*the whole flag*] would be a dollar.
Colin:	Once you add a quarter to another quarter, it keeps getting bigger and bigger and bigger.
Teacher:	Ah. Colin is saying something a little different.
Joshua:	Do you mean a money quarter or do you mean a quarter of the rectangle?
Teacher:	Hold on. Colin is saying that when you add a quarter to another quarter, it gets bigger and bigger.
Reed:	Oh, because why it got bigger is because there's a bunch of quarters that makes the halves.
Teacher:	It makes two halves? Oh, all these quarters together make two halves?
Reed:	Yeah.

We talked a little bit more while other children worked to make sense of this idea that a quarter (25¢) was really one-fourth of a dollar. I can see that this is really confusing. It's the same word, and it means the same thing in reference to a dollar, but it is something of its own as well: an object whose name is a "quarter."

Sadie then drew our attention back to the flag of Nigeria. She said you could cut the flag in half, and then you'd have a third and part of a third. Reed said that if you drew a line down the middle of the green part, it makes a fourth. So I drew this out for the class and asked if the new parts were all quarters.

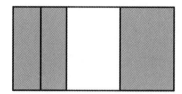

The class responded with a resounding no. Sadie said that each part would be a sixth. She pointed to each section as she counted: "1 [*the first small green section*], 2 [*the second small green section*], 3, 4 [*the white section*], 5, 6 [*the last green section*]." She concluded, "Each one is a sixth." 370

> **Teacher:** Do you want me to split up the others?
>
> **Cloe:** It's not even if you don't split up the other ones.

Cloe and Sadie talked a bit more, and I asked someone to restate what they were saying. 375

> **Clara:** If they aren't all the same size, then they aren't all the same.
>
> **Teacher:** That's what we were saying the other day, that they have to be equal pieces, right?

We finished the conversation with some other observations, and the children went on to the paper part of the activity, filling in their new set of flags. 380

I am left thinking again about this sense of sameness or "equal-ness" that they are bringing to their fraction work and how those images will serve them as they move on to harder fraction work in future years. In fact, I wonder how all of these images will serve them, including Colin's image of fractions being connected to money. 384

5

Combining shares, or adding fractions

In chapter 1 you read cases describing students' work in whole number addition and subtraction. In this chapter, we return to addition, but now we examine students who are working on adding fractions.

- What do we learn about the meaning of addition when we explore the complexities of adding fractions?

- What must we understand about fractions in order to figure out how to add them?

case 22

Sharing brownies or adding fractions

MaryAnn
GRADE 4, FEBRUARY

When my colleague, Janie, gave me her Problem of the Week last week, I felt that it would fit right in with what my class was doing with fractions. Each week, Janie picks a problem and distributes it to all the staff at our school—teachers, administrators, support staff—everyone. And lots of people work on it. Our staff development coordinator has declared herself "math phobic," but she works on the problem every week and is determined to learn how to solve problems like these. Even the custodian submits his solution each week. Some of the teachers give the problems to their students.

Anyway, this particular problem came from *Seeing Fractions: A Unit for the Upper Elementary Grades* (California Department of Education 1990; developed by TERC). It reads as follows:

> I invited 8 people to my party (including me) and I only had 3 brownies. How much did each person get if they had fair shares?
>
> We were still hungry, and I finally found 2 more brownies in the bottom of the cookie jar. They were stale, but we ate them anyway. This time, how much did each person get?
>
> How much brownie in all did each person eat?

The problem is quite a bit more complex than those we had been working on. I don't think I would have chosen this problem on my own, but since it arrived in my mailbox, I decided to give it a try. I wondered what my students would do with it.

We have spent three days of math class on the problem. The children worked on their own or in pairs, as they chose, while I moved around the room holding discussions to see how they understood the problem. Sometimes, I asked the children to share their strategies with the rest of the class. Now, on this third day, I'm looking over their written work.

Although everybody wrote something that related to fractions, a couple of children didn't pick up on the concept of *fair shares*. They took the 3 brownies, broke them into 8 pieces, and wrote out $\frac{1}{2} + \frac{1}{2} + \frac{1}{2} + \frac{1}{2} + \frac{1}{4} + \frac{1}{4} + \frac{1}{4} + \frac{1}{4}$. They felt satisfied that this was a solution to the problem.

Most of the children did come up with a valid answer to each of the three questions. I am quite interested in Maribel's work. She has devised a procedure that she applies to all cases of fair shares: Cut the brownies so that each person gets one piece from each brownie. For example, to answer the first question, she drew 8 faces for the 8 people at the party and drew

5

10

15

20

25

30

3 brownies, which she cut into eighths. She then began distributing the pieces to the people. Each time she distributed 8 pieces, she crossed out the brownie they came from. After she finished distributing the pieces, she counted them up. "They each get $^3/_8$," she wrote. Maribel 35 then applied the same procedure to answer the second question, concluding, "They each get $^2/_8$."

Looking at Maribel's work on the first two questions (fig. 5.1), I would have expected her to say something like, "If they first got $^3/_8$ and then later got $^2/_8$, that means that they got $^5/_8$ all together." But that's not what she did. Instead, she treated the third question as if it were a completely new problem: 8 people shared 5 brownies. She drew her 8 faces and drew her 40 5 brownies and applied the same procedure again (fig. 5.2). There's certainly nothing incorrect about her procedure, and she felt satisfied with her answer of $^5/_8$. I wonder if she recognizes that she could have solved the problem by adding.

Fig. 5.1. Maribel's work on the first two parts of the Brownie problem   45

Fig. 5.2. Maribel's work on the third question in the Brownie problem

Alejandro used a method common to several other students in the class. He first saw that 2 brownies could be distributed among 8 people if you cut them into fourths, and he drew out the 8 quarter-portions. The third brownie could be cut into eighths, so for each person he drew an eighth next to the fourth. He concluded, "First they got ¹/₄ and ¹/₈." For the second part of the problem, he again distributed the 2 brownies by cutting them into fourths, drawing in another quarter-portion for each person: "Then they got ¹/₄." Looking at his pictorial representation, Alejandro concluded, "Altogether they got ²/₄ and ¹/₈." He also drew a brownie and shaded in ¹/₄ and ¹/₄ and ¹/₈ (fig. 5.3).

I feel quite satisfied with the work of the children who solved the problem the way Alejandro did, but I still have questions about what they are thinking. In the brownie at the lower right of Alejandro's page, which he divided into 8 eighths, each of the parts labeled ¹/₄ pretty clearly shows ²/₈. Can he look at his drawing and see that ¹/₄ = ²/₈? Can he see that he has shaded in ⁵/₈? Does he see that, when Maribel says each person ate ⁵/₈ of a brownie, her answer represents the same amount as his? I expect to have opportunities in the coming days to follow up these questions about what my students are thinking.

Usually I distribute my time pretty evenly among my students, asking them questions while they are working. Sometimes, however, I give more of my time to children who especially need

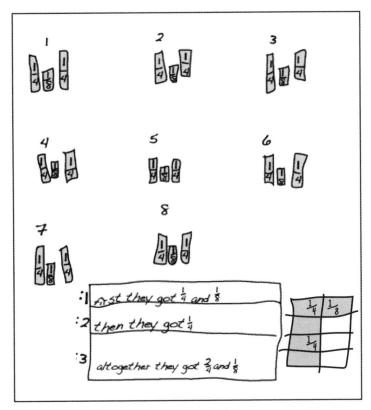

Fig. 5.3. Alejandro's work on the Brownie problem

attention; then I catch up with the others later. During the three days that we worked on this   65
problem, I spent much of my time with Jackson.

Jackson is a sweet kid who is almost always disorganized. At the beginning of the school
year, I found it hard to listen to him; he always seemed to be rambling, and it was difficult to
make sense of what he was saying. His classmates seemed to have the same reaction. However,
in recent years I have learned to listen hard for the ideas my students are trying to express, and   70
when I persevered, I found that listening to Jackson offered unexpected rewards. He has good
mathematical insights. And when I listen hard and take seriously what Jackson is saying, so do
his classmates. Their relationship to him has improved since September.

On the day that I handed out the problem, I moved through the classroom, looking over
children's shoulders, pausing to listen to their conversations, sometimes asking them questions   75
so that I could better understand what they were thinking. By the time I got to Jackson, he had
answers for all three questions. However, his page was so messy, I couldn't interpret what he
had done (fig. 5.4). When I asked him to explain, he could share some confident and correct
thinking. Yet, as he tried to retrace what he had done, he lost track of his thinking and couldn't
make sense of his own disorganized written work.   80

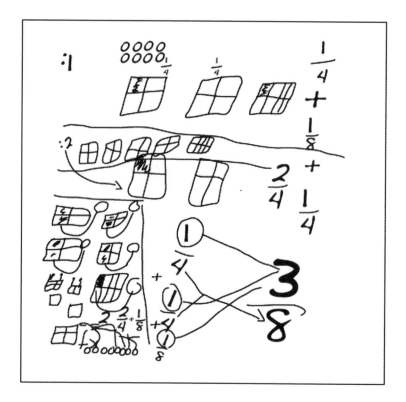

Fig. 5.4. Jackson's work on the Brownie question, day 1

For the first question, Jackson was able to explain quickly that 3 brownies had been cut up so that 8 people each received $1/4$ from the first two brownies and then received $1/8$ from the third. He noted that each fair share was $1/4 + 1/8$. (Unlike Alejandro, Jackson used the plus sign instead of the word *and*.)

Jackson's illustration for the second question showed 2 brownies cut into 8 equal shares of $1/4$ each. His answer to the second question was $1/4$.

The third part got very messy. Unfortunately for Jackson, much good thinking gets lost because of his poor organizational skills. It was difficult for him to figure out what he had done in this section. He knew what the question was, but he seemed to feel that he had to reconstruct the whole problem before he could reach a conclusion. (This is what Maribel had done, too.) I wonder why he didn't realize that he had already figured out much of what he needed to know and that he just needed to use the information from the first two parts.

When Jackson worked to distribute 5 brownies among 8 people, he figured that they got $1/4$ and $1/4$ and $1/8$. We can see on his paper that he wrote $1/4 + 1/4 + 1/8$ in a vertical column and came up with an answer of $3/8$.

At this point, it appeared that Jackson had separated the numbers from the problem context. When I asked him how he got $3/8$, he explained that he added the 1s (the numerators) and then added $4 + 4$, two of the denominators, to get 8. He decided that since the other denominator is also 8, it stays the same, "So $3/8$." Jackson wanted to be satisfied with this answer and wanted

85

90

95

100

me to leave him alone. Instead, I asked him to think about the third part of the problem and told him we'd talk about it again later. This was the end of the first day.

The next day I had some of the children share their solutions on the board. Jackson came to the board to talk about the third question (fig. 5.5). 105

Fig. 5.5. Jackson's board work explaining his solution to the Brownie problem, day 2

Jackson: All right, draw 5 brownies, like this. [*He draws 5 squares.*] Cut the first two into 4 parts each [*which he does*], and then make the next one into 8 parts. [*Without speaking, he also divides the last two squares into eighths.*] 110

Although I knew that this would work out OK, I wondered aloud why he had changed his strategy from yesterday's attempt. He shrugged. Then he counted up what each person got and came up with an answer $1/4$ and $3/8$. This time he didn't try to combine them to create a single fractional number.

I was struck by the clarity of Jackson's presentation. Although he frequently loses focus 115 when working with complex problems, once focused, he can confidently arrive at an accurate solution.

However, our work on the problem—and my thinking about Jackson—wasn't done. The next day, we continued the group discussion about the children's various solutions. When one child said that he didn't understand what Jackson had done, Jackson offered to explain it again, 120 one-on-one. I was interested to hear how he would rephrase the problem and his solution, so I listened in.

Jackson showed how the first 3 brownies could be distributed among 8 people to make portions of $1/4 + 1/8$ (fig. 5.6). He then showed how the next 2 brownies would give each person $1/4$. I noted that he had gone back to his original strategy. And then, Jackson began to work on the 125 third question without redoing the entire problem; he seemed to realize that the answer could be derived from the first two parts. He came up with answer of $1/4 + 1/4 + 1/8 = 3/8$. I wanted to hear more.

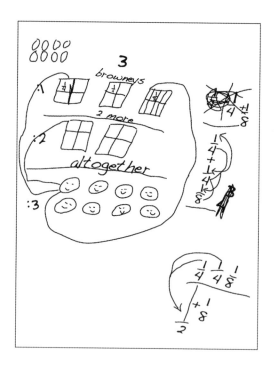

Fig. 5.6. Jackson's attempt to explain his solution to a classmate, day 3

Teacher: I see that you did some work with the fractions over here. [*I point to some crossed-out figures on his paper.*] I'm wondering why you crossed out some numbers. 130

Jackson: I was adding the 1 + 1 + 1 and it came to 3, but then I went to add the bottoms [4 + 4 + 8] and it didn't make sense. There's nothing here that's 16, and the numbers I was getting wouldn't match the brownies. When I looked at the brownies, I could see that each person had ¹/₄ and ¹/₄ and ¹/₈, and I know the ¹/₄ 135 and ¹/₄ make ¹/₂, and then ¹/₈. So, I'm telling you each person had a share of ¹/₂ and ¹/₈.

Jackson had come up with three different correct representations for a single fair share in this problem:

$$\tfrac{1}{4} + \tfrac{1}{4} + \tfrac{1}{8} \qquad \tfrac{1}{4} \text{ and } \tfrac{3}{8} \qquad \tfrac{1}{2} \text{ and } \tfrac{1}{8}$$
140

I wonder how he perceives Alejandro's ²/₄ and ¹/₈ or Maribel's answer of ⁵/₈.

This is a question I will pose to the class tomorrow. Are these the same amount or different amounts? Can they all be solutions to the same problem? 143

case 23

How many ways can you add $\frac{1}{3}$ to $\frac{1}{4}$? Or interesting stuff happens!

Henry
GRADE 6, DECEMBER

This year I teach sixth-grade math to three different groups each day. I have found that the more control I assume and structure I apply the more similar the three classes will be on a given day. When I give up some of that control and allow the students to voice their ideas, the groups move in divergent directions.

A recent lesson looked quite simple in my plan book. We had been adding fractions with like denominators and had begun to get ready to deal with unlike denominators. We had experimented with finding common multiples, explored equivalency, practiced simplifying fractions, and begun changing fractions to higher terms.

I was feeling that we were in the thick of a computational jungle, and I wanted us to look at some concepts together. I also wanted to get an idea of what my students were thinking. For my lesson, I asked the students to make pictures (diagrams) of what is happening when we add $\frac{1}{3}$ to $\frac{1}{4}$. Each class handled it very differently.

In the first class, I started out by asking the group to draw what happens when we add $\frac{1}{3}$ to $\frac{1}{3}$. Alexandra came to the board to show us her picture. She drew it out this way:

first $\frac{1}{3}$ second $\frac{1}{3}$

$\frac{1}{3}$	$\frac{1}{3}$	

This seemed quite straightforward; no one offered a different notion or any objections. Thinking that this was just how I saw it, I plowed forward with the main lesson, asking the class to work in groups to draw a picture of $\frac{1}{3} + \frac{1}{4}$. (There were a few other instructions, too, such as create a story problem to accompany the numbers, and explain your group's picture and approach to another group, but for this case I am focusing on the pictures they drew.)

All groups used Alexandra's work as a model, and although there were certainly some moments of struggle, groups produced this type of drawing:

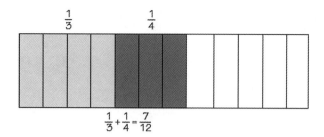

When asked how exactly they came up with the twelfths, they answered that they "found a common denominator and changed to higher terms" and so on. In other words, they mimicked the computation we had been doing in the previous days and did not look beneath the computational surface of the problem. It wasn't really their fault either, for this is sort of what I expected, what I wanted. This was an obvious reaction to what I had set up. 170

The second class began with the same instructions; however, our model student, Ramón, opened up a mathematical Pandora's box with his drawing of $1/3 + 1/3$:

175

He explained this was equal to $2/3$, but Tanya wondered, "Isn't that really equal to 2 out of 6 or $2/6$, which is just $1/3$? But how could $1/3 + 1/3 = 1/3$?"

In trying to sort this out, Colin came up with the following illustration:

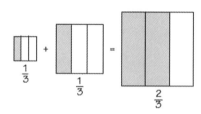

Of course the different size wholes then brought up other issues. Ten minutes into this lesson I had discovered that a good deal of confusion lived just beneath the surface—not the computational surface, but the conceptual one. I know that it was there in the first class, too, but I just wasn't able to get it to bubble up. 180

For the third class, I completely abandoned my preconceived plans and expectations. I decided to do away with the model example of $1/3 + 1/3$ and to start with $1/3 + 1/4$. I asked the students to try not to think about any computational angles, but to attempt to picture their understanding. This approach yielded entirely different results. Lizette showed this diagram to get started on $1/3 + 1/4$: 185

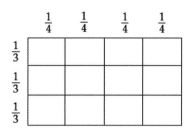

3 rows by 4 columns = twelfths   190

We began to investigate if this type of picture would be a good way to come up with a lowest common multiple for two numbers. The conversations and investigations were lively. In the midst of it all, some kids were doing exactly what I do when I am involved in similar situations as a student. They were "doing their own thing," going off on tangents, discovering ideas that have been experienced by others millions of times but were new to them. Why didn't this environment exist in the other two classes? I wondered and still wonder. I'm sure that much of the answer is that I did not allow it to exist, or to put it more mildly, I did not effectively sponsor it.

As this class ended, one student, Ming-hua, came up to show me that he had discovered something cool:

200

$$\frac{1}{3}$$
$$+\frac{1}{4}$$
$$\frac{7}{12} \quad \text{because it's} \quad \frac{3+4}{3\times 4}$$

$$\frac{1}{15}$$
$$+\frac{1}{2}$$
$$\frac{17}{30} \quad \text{because it's} \quad \frac{15+2}{15\times 2}$$

My reaction to Ming-hua? "WOW!"

In conclusion, what does it all mean? Honestly, I'm not sure. I know that does not establish closure, so … I guess it means that the teacher sets the tone for the lesson and the environment of the class consciously but oftentimes unconsciously, too. When I don't expect my students to be clones of me and merely follow my lead, when I genuinely listen to their questions and don't   205
rush to answer them, interesting stuff happens.   206

case 24

"Doling out" and fractions

Greta
GRADES 6 AND 7 (SPECIAL ED), NOVEMBER

I have been thinking about how my students use "doling" as a strategy for solving division problems of whole numbers with the remainder expressed as a fraction. The strategy of doling out has its pros and cons. On the upside, doling is very systematic and easy to understand. On the downside, some of my students can't reassemble all the fractional pieces into just one fraction. For others the equivalency issue is akin to changing the problem. 210

For example, consider one boy's approach to this problem:

Four kids share 19 pizzas. How much will each kid get? 215

Gunther will dole out all the wholes first: The 4 kids each get 4 whole pizzas. Then taking the 3 remaining pizzas, he will cut 2 of them in half, dole out each $\frac{1}{2}$, then cut the last pizza in 4 pieces and dole out $\frac{1}{4}$ to each kid. Gunther writes as his answer: "The first boy gets 4 wholes and $\frac{1}{2}$ and $\frac{1}{4}$. The second boy gets 4 wholes and $\frac{1}{2}$ and $\frac{1}{4}$. The third boy gets …," and so on. Gunther is very systematic in breaking down the pizza into ever smaller pieces. But 220 when Mercedes says that her answer of $4\frac{3}{4}$ is the same as his, he initially objects. She shows him how his half pieces can be cut into fourths. "But I know I got the answer; this changes my drawing," he protests. There are two underlying issues for him, I think: He doesn't yet know that mixed numbers are conventionally expressed as a whole and one fraction and that fractional pieces like $\frac{1}{2}$ and $\frac{1}{4}$ can be added. 225

Another boy handled the following problem in an interesting way:

Three kids share 1 stick of gum. How much does each get?

Dominic wrote:

$\frac{4}{4}$ equals 1 whole. So we divide it into four parts: $\frac{1}{4}$, $\frac{2}{4}$, $\frac{3}{4}$, $\frac{4}{4}$. Each kid is going to get $\frac{1}{4}$. So $\frac{3}{4}$ are gone. [There] is $\frac{1}{4}$ left so we need to divide $\frac{1}{4}$ into $\frac{1}{12}$ pieces. [Each kid 230 gets] $\frac{1}{4}$ and $\frac{1}{12}$.

Dominic's drawing first looked as shown at left; then he extended the three horizontal lines to make twelfths (right).

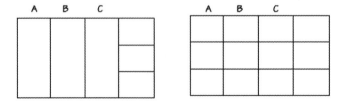

While showing and describing his work, Dominic realized that $^1/_4$ and $^1/_{12}$ could also be   235
called $^4/_{12}$. When I asked if there was an easier way to do this problem, Dominic returned with a
drawing showing thirds:

Dominic's work is shown in figure 5.7.

Dominic, like Gunther, would have left his answer as $^1/_4 + ^1/_{12}$, except that our conversation   240
about his drawing led him to the other answer. Again I started thinking about how students
sometimes shy away from combining fractional pieces on the initial solution.

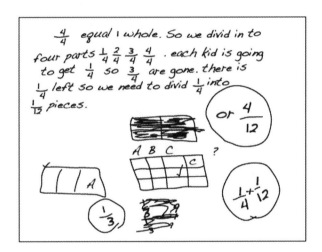

Fig. 5.7. Dominic's work showing how 3 kids share 1 stick of gum

In another problem of this type, 9 kids shared 21 pizzas. How much did each get? For this   245
problem, some students chose to use small plastic circles to represent the pizzas. Antonio was
able to dole out 2 circles for each of the 9 kids. Then on the "leftover" 3 circles, he drew lines on
the plastic and numbered 9 slices. When asked about his work, Antonio explained that each kid
got 2 wholes and $^1/_9$ and $^1/_9$ and $^1/_9$. However, while he worked on recording his ideas on paper
(fig. 5.8), he forgot how many ninths each kid got and gave 2 and $^1/_9$ as his answer.   250

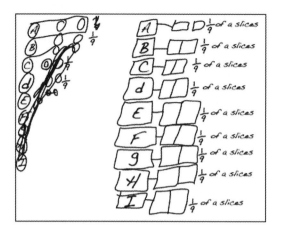

Fig. 5.8. After using plastic circles to solve the sharing of 21 pizzas among 9 kids, Antonio tried to represent his work on paper.

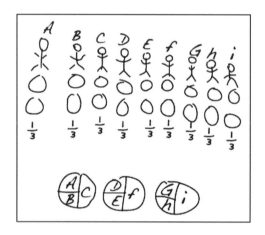

Fig. 5.9. In Zoe's work, she first doles out 18 pizzas and then divides the 3 leftover pizzas into thirds.

On the same problem Zoe showed an impressive ability to keep straight in her head a lot of information. She laid out 36 plastic circles in a 9-by-4 array. I thought that she was totally confused. She proved me wrong. She told me the first row across was the 9 kids. The next 2 rows were the wholes. The bottom row was the thirds. I was amazed because all the circles were identical. When she worked on paper (fig. 5.9), Zoe represented the kids, whole pizzas, and thirds differently. That was less confusing for me.

255

260

262

Taking portions of portions, or multiplying fractions

In chapter 2, you read cases describing students' work in whole number multiplication and division. In this chapter, we examine students who are working on multiplying fractions.

- What sorts of situations could be modeled by, say, $1/3 \times 1/4$, and what is it about such situations that make multiplication appropriate?
- What representations are especially useful for depicting multiplication of fractions?

case 25

Clock faces and equivalence

Ann
GRADE 6, NOVEMBER

As my sixth-grade students explored equivalent fractions, I used a lesson from *Rectangles, Clocks, and Tracks*, a unit from *Investigations in Number, Data, and Space*, (3rd ed., Pearson 2016). It asked the students to look at clock faces and determine what portion of the clock face the hour hand has passed through since 12 o'clock (fig. 6.1). I have come to expect the unexpected when conducting a math lesson, and this lesson was no exception.

Jaclyn started with the clock reading 1 o'clock. "I think it's $1/12$ because there are 12 parts and 1 of them is being used."

Rusty chimed in, "It could be $5/60$, too, because there are 60 minutes in an hour and 5 minutes are the portion shown."

Midori suggested, "It could be $2/24$ because that is equal to $1/12$."

"What portion would $1/24$ represent on the clock?" I asked.

Liam raised his hand. "It would be $2\frac{1}{2}$ minutes, because $2/24$ is 5 minutes, so half of 5 minutes is $2\frac{1}{2}$ minutes."

I asked if there were any other ideas, and Amini spoke up: "It could also be 1/3 of 1/4 of the clock face."

This response initially brought puzzled looks and questions to the other students and to me. What was Amini seeing? First he was looking at the whole clock face and breaking it into quarters; then looking at just the one quarter, he noticed that a third of it was the portion marked. This ability to look at a portion of a portion was unexpected.

As we looked at the other clock faces, students continued to point out this portion-of-a-portion equivalency. Ferris said that the clock face showing 2 o'clock was 2 of 1. For 3 o'clock, Liam said the portion shown was $1/6$ plus $1/2$ of $1/6$. Ferris suggested that we could also call it $1/2$ of $1/2$. Midori saw 4 o'clock as $4/6$ of $1/2$. Similar examples happened on each clock face.

Not all students were able to see these equivalencies. What is necessary for a student—or a teacher—to see them? I speculate that one must be able to identify the whole first. In this case, the clock face was the whole. After recognizing this, you have to notice a portion of the whole, such as $1/2$ or $1/4$, and have *this* become the "whole" you focus on for a while—but you still need to hold onto its relationship with the whole clock face. You then compare the new whole ($1/2$ or $1/4$, for example) to the portion indicated by the hour hand. Is the hour hand's movement a sixth of the new portion, a half of it, a third of it? To do this, someone must be able to see relationships within relationships. I feel that this is a big mathematical issue for my students.

Fig. 6.1. Clock Fractions from grade 5, unit 4, *What's That Portion?* in TERC's *Investigations in Number, Data, and Space* (2008), Pearson Education

35

case 26

Multiplication of mixed numbers

Sarita
GRADE 6, NOVEMBER

I asked the students in my sixth-grade class to solve the following problem by drawing a large, clearly labeled picture:

> What is the area of a rectangle that has a width of 2³/₄ units and a length of 3²/₃ units?   40

As I was walking around the classroom, listening to and observing students working on the problem, I overheard the following comment:

Yuri: Usually all you have to do to find the area is to multiply the length times the width, but because we have fractions, you can't do that.   45

We had spent weeks working on area and perimeter problems, so the students were familiar with finding the area of a region by counting the number of units or, in the case of rectangles, by multiplying the width times the length. Why did Yuri think this method would not apply with fractions?

When we started the whole-group discussion, Olivia volunteered to come to the board and   50
discuss her strategy for solving the problem. She carefully drew her picture on the board.

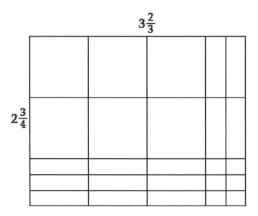

Olivia: You can get some of the area but not all of it.

Teacher: What part of the area can you get?

Olivia: I know that the length times the width is the area, so 2 × 3 = 6.   55

Teacher: Where is the 2 × 3, or the 6, in the picture?

Olivia:	The big squares are the wholes and you can just count 6. The smaller pieces you can count, too, but they don't count as wholes.
Teacher:	Why not?
Olivia:	Those pieces aren't whole squares the way that the other ones are because of the fractions. So [*counting to herself*], there are 4 of those [she points to the rectangles at the top right], and that is $1^1/_3$. If you put 4 fourths together [*pointing to the larger rectangles at the bottom*], that's 2 wholes and $^1/_4$ left. But I don't know how to count the other pieces.
Teacher:	Why not?
Olivia:	They are like pieces of pieces of something.
Kyle:	Like fractions of pieces when the pieces are fractions.

There was a pause in the class as they mulled that one over. Then there was a flutter of voices as the children talked to one another. I let them discuss this for a minute or two.

Teacher:	Can someone paraphrase what Kyle said?
Shantea:	I think he is saying that those pieces are fractions of fractions, but what is that anyway?
Meryl:	There is $^2/_3$ on one side and $^3/_4$ on the other side.
Geraldo:	Almost like $^2/_3$ of $^3/_4$, but that's not possible.
Cecilia:	Yeah! No way could you have $^2/_3$ of $^3/_4$!

At this point I decided to introduce an idea that might ease the struggle that the students were having. I used the example that Geraldo and another student had posed, but I put the idea into a simple and meaningful context.

Teacher:	Think about this. Someone gave me $^3/_4$ of a leftover candy bar. [*I drew a diagram on the board.*] I ate $^2/_3$ of that for lunch. What part of the whole candy bar did I eat?

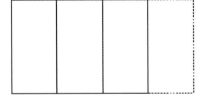

Maurice:	$^2/_3$ of $^3/_4$. That's got to be $^6/_{12}$. Just put some lines here, and you can see the $^6/_{12}$. [*He adds two horizontal lines to my diagram and shades in a portion showing $^2/_3$ of $^3/_4$.*] And $^6/_{12}$ is the same as $^1/_2$.

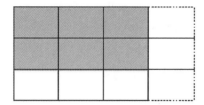

Felicia: He's right!

Mario said he saw the ²/₃ as two of the three pieces of the leftover candy bar (in the original diagram), which he could then see was half of the whole candy bar.

90

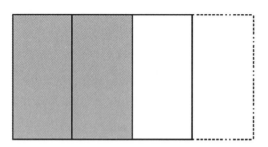

Students discussed this information until the idea was more comfortable for them. They returned to the original problem and decided that we could indeed find the area of the entire region by taking all the things that we had counted and adding them together. They added unlike denominators by using Olivia's picture and thinking about equivalent fractions as they worked through the numbers.

95

At the end of class, Basimah was busy studying Olivia's picture on the board.

Basimah: You know, another way to look at this would be to extend the picture, to show the missing parts of the pieces of pieces. That way we could just see what they were. [*She extended the original diagram as she had proposed.*] Then you know that the pieces are twelfths, and you can count them the way you   100 can count the rest of the pieces.

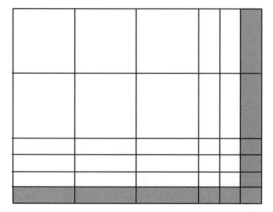

She was absolutely right! I asked her why she hadn't shared that with the class, and she said that she just now discovered it by looking at the picture.

After class, I reflected on the students' method to solve the problem I had posed. My goal is   105
that the students, at some point, will develop an arithmetic algorithm from their picture. When I examine the diagram, I recognize a procedure based on subproducts, much like the basic principle that underlies most common algorithms for multiplying multi-digit whole numbers.

To multiply $2^3/_4 \times 3^2/_3$, find the subproducts:

$2 \times 3 = 6$ 110
$2 \times {}^2/_3 = {}^4/_3 = 1^1/_3$
$3 \times {}^3/_4 = {}^9/_4 = 2^1/_4$
${}^2/_3 \times {}^3/_4 = {}^6/_{12}$

Then add all the parts:

$6 + 1^1/_3 + 2^1/_4 + {}^6/_{12} = 10^1/_{12}$ 115

This works, and seems very clear. But the procedure presented in most middle-grade mathematics texts involves changing mixed numbers to improper fractions, multiplying, and then changing the answer back to a mixed number.

$2^3/_4 \times 3^2/_3 =$
${}^{11}/_4 \times {}^{11}/_3 =$ 120
${}^{121}/_{12} = 10^1/_2$

When I looked for these numbers in the picture, I found them by drawing more lines so that I could transform everything into fourths and thirds. By making darker lines to keep straight what stood for 1, I could then see how the twelfths appear.

125

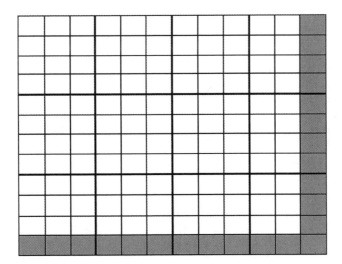

Now that I understand this better for myself, I still need to think through my goals for my students.   127

case 27

What I want my students to understand about multiplication

Henry
GRADE 6, DECEMBER

"What is it you want your students to understand?" has been asked of me so often over the two years since I've been in this professional development project that I now automatically ask the question of myself. This represents a change, because I used to set my goals by thinking "these are the things I want my students to be able to do"—not unlike trained seals. My students could move numbers around and about; understanding was expected to come as part of the package. However, I'm not sure I ever knew exactly what I wanted them to understand. This is my attempt to nail down a few ideas about multiplication.

1. *Multiplication does not always make things bigger.*

   Whole number multiplication leaves students with some observations and assumptions that do not hold water when decimals and fractions float by. This is one big misconception.

2. *Multiplication is not just repeated addition.*

   The link between multiplication and addition seemed to make great sense with whole number problems, but multiplication is a great deal more complex than just repeated addition.

3. *What is the mystery of "times"?*

   Many of my students read 7 × 9 as "7 times 9" but have no idea what that means. Times seems to be an unfathomable word to some of them.

4. *3 × 4 = 4 × 3, but are they the same?*

   So many of my students seem "answer driven," and the notion that multiplication is commutative makes good and easy sense to them. But 3 groups of 4 is different from 4 groups of 3.

[oooo]	[ooo]
[oooo]	[ooo]
[oooo]	[ooo]
	[ooo]

130

135

140

145

150

5. *How do you translate a multiplication expression, and can you understand what it means?*

The expression 5×6 could be 5 groups of 6, or it could be 5 taken 6 times. This interchangeable nature stretches a bit too far when students attempt to make sense of $1/2 \times 1/4$. The idea of "$1/2$ taken $1/4$ at a time" is of little value. Thinking about "$1/2$ group of $1/4$." makes better sense, but this, too, is not easy to understand. Drawings and pictures can greatly help understanding, at least when they aren't causing more confusion. My sense is that confusion in these areas—translating the multiplication equation into something understandable, and being able to represent that understanding in a picture form—is desirable, for without that confusion, students will not achieve that understanding. And I think that understanding this stuff is key to understanding multiplication itself.

155

160

6. *The numbers in a multiplication equation are connected to real things.*

I want my students to be aware that numbers don't always exist by themselves—they are useful representations of things, such as people, money, or objects. And they help us solve real-world problems. I have found that when students make the connection between realistic problems and multiplication equations, the operation of multiplication becomes clearer, and many of the misconceptions that exist when dealing only with numbers pose no threat.

165

170

7. *Students should not be hypnotized by numbers.*

A student will work with a problem like $3\frac{1}{2} \times 3\frac{1}{2}$ and get an answer such as 37, or perhaps $2\frac{1}{4}$. These answers are outrageously incorrect, but many times we become blinded while computing numbers and fail to think about what those numbers mean. I want my students to realize that $3\frac{1}{2} \times 3\frac{1}{2}$ can't possibly equal more than 4×4 or less than 3×3. Estimation is a useful tool.

175

8. *There is a real connection between multiplication and division.*

Students seem to recite automatically that multiplication and division are opposites, and leave it at that. But to truly understand that $10 \times 1/2 = 10 \div 2$ and to contend with other similar problems, it seems necessary to dig a little deeper. And there's mathematical gold to be found here, for stuff like reciprocals and division of fractions can then be seen in a different way.

180

Since I am sure there are more important ideas about multiplication that I have not yet touched on, I will leave this unfinished.

184

Expanding ideas about division in the context of fractions

The cases in chapter 7 present the work of two sixth-grade classes as they solve problems that their teachers identify as division of fractions. These cases not only provide us an opportunity to study division of fractions for ourselves but they also return us to the themes of this seminar:

- What does it mean to model a situation with a piece of arithmetic?
- As we see the various number sentences that could represent a single situation, what do we learn about the operations?
- How are our ideas about the operations extended as we encounter new situations they might model?

case 28

Who says that's not the right equation? My own experience vs. students' thinking

Sarita
GRADE 6, MAY

The students in my sixth-grade class have been solving fraction word problems for several weeks. Today they were spread around the classroom, working in groups of twos and threes. The directions were to draw a picture to solve the problem, write a number sentence (equation) that explains the problem, and show any computation. This was the problem I gave them to   5
solve:

> You are giving a party. You have 6 pints of ice cream for the party. If you serve
> $3/4$ of a pint of ice cream to each guest, how many guests can be served?

For the most part, the students didn't find this a difficult problem. They drew pictures to represent the pints of ice cream and separated each pint into 4 equal sections. They explained   10
that every 3 sections were what one person would receive, and that was equal to $3/4$. There was enough to do that 8 times, so 6 pints would serve 8 people.

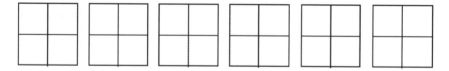

However, when they expressed this problem in a number sentence or equation, the range of answers was interesting. I use the word interesting because I am not sure whether or not   15
the students are incorrect or they just see things differently. Although I could understand the thinking behind their equations, I didn't think that they were "correct." I had been taught that equations have to match what is going on in the problem. In my mind the students' equations were, though not necessarily wrong, not quite correct, either.

I was trying to get the students to see that the problem could be solved by $6 \div 3/4$. Instead, they   20
came up with the following equations and had impressive reasoning to justify their thinking:

Equation	Justification
$24 \div 3 = 8$	There are 24 pieces, 3 pieces to a serving, 8 people can be served.
$8 \times \frac{3}{4} = 6$	8 servings of $\frac{3}{4}$ of a pint each gives you 6 whole pints.
$\frac{3}{4} + \frac{3}{4} + \frac{3}{4} + \frac{3}{4} +$ $\frac{3}{4} + \frac{3}{4} + \frac{3}{4} + \frac{3}{4} = 6$	$\frac{3}{4}$ each gives you 6 whole pints.
$6 - \frac{3}{4} - \frac{3}{4} - \frac{3}{4} - \frac{3}{4} -$ $\frac{3}{4} - \frac{3}{4} - \frac{3}{4} - \frac{3}{4} = 0$	Take $\frac{3}{4}$ pint for each serving. You can do this 8 times.

Students also presented some other equations along with those listed above. Our routine is to leave all ideas out for discussion until the students are sure that a particular idea doesn't make sense. Thus, the following equations remained on the board even though I could not accept their logic.   25

Equation	Justification
$8 \div \frac{1}{4} = 6$	8 people were served, they had 6 pints, and the picture shows fourths.
$6 \div \frac{1}{4} = 8$	[This was proposed in response to students who insisted that they couldn't accept the previous equation.]
$24 \div \frac{3}{4} = 8$ or 6	There are 24 pieces altogether, and each serving is $\frac{3}{4}$ of a pint, so there are 6 pints or 8 servings (depending on what you are looking for).
$\frac{3}{4} \div 8 = 6$	$\frac{3}{4}$ pint is the serving, there are 6 pints of ice cream, so 8 servings.

These last few equations do not make sense mathematically, nor do the justifications help them make sense. In some ways these were the easy equations to dismiss. For the last one, I might be persuaded to help this student reexamine whole number division, because the justification seems clear—it just doesn't go with the equation. 30

My dilemma is that the first set of equations does not feel "right" to me even though they make mathematical sense. The $24 \div 3 = 8$ is disturbing. I see what the students mean, and I understand what they are doing; but these are whole numbers, and I think this is a fraction problem. Can it be both? 35

Where do I go from here? What do I do with my own thinking? What do I do to get the students to see this as a fraction division problem? Or do I? Who is confused, the students or me? 38

case 29

Stretching elastic

Selena
GRADE 6, NOVEMBER

40

For a recent homework assignment, students were asked to solve a problem by drawing a diagram and writing an equation. When they arrived in mathematics class the next day, I placed them randomly in groups of two or three for a discussion of how everyone in their group solved the problem. Part of the homework asked for alternative solutions to the problem, so students knew that listening to other people's ideas would help them finish the worksheet. They also knew that I would then select a group of students to come to the board to explain how they solved the problem. This was the problem we were working on:

45

> A piece of elastic can be stretched to $5\frac{1}{2}$ times its original length. When fully stretched, it is 33 meters long. What was the elastic's original length?

The first group to come to the board solved the problem with the following diagrams, first showing the length of the stretched elastic:

50

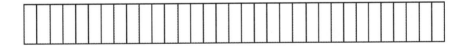

Marcus: This is the 33 meters. We want to put them in $5\frac{1}{2}$ groups.

The group proceeded to separate the 33 meters of elastic into sections $5\frac{1}{2}$ meters long.

55

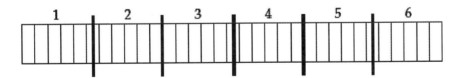

Before they could continue, hands all around the room flew into the air. Marcus called on Deena.

Deena: I agree with the 6, but I disagree with what Marcus said.

Teacher: What do you mean?

Deena: I know what Marcus is doing, but I think he is all mixed up.

60

Teacher: Can you say more about that?

I was not sure what Deena was thinking or what she was trying to articulate. It was difficult for her to express what she meant, but I wanted to give her the opportunity to explain her ideas.

Deena: OK. The 6 is the answer. I know that because there are 6 groups. Marcus said that they put the 33 meters into $5\frac{1}{2}$ groups, but they didn't do that.   65

Teacher: Can someone tell us in other words what Deena is saying?

Amir: I think Deena is saying that Marcus's group said one thing but did another. It doesn't really matter.

Patrice: But if it doesn't matter, where did the 6 come from anyway? You don't know about the 6 until you solve the problem.   70

Francine: [*She is Marcus's partner.*] We didn't know about the 6 until we finished with the groups. I think Marcus meant to say that we kept counting $5\frac{1}{2}$ pieces, or meters, until we ran out of meters. When we finished, we had 6 as the answer.

Teacher: Six what?

Marcus: Six meters. I see what they mean though. I didn't make $5\frac{1}{2}$ groups; I made 6 groups of $5\frac{1}{2}$.   75

Teacher: Can the problem be solved if we made $5\frac{1}{2}$ groups?

The students quickly discussed this question and began drawing new diagrams on their papers. Many were excited to think that I might have provided them with the alternative solution they were required to include on their homework papers.   80

I wondered if the students would be able to think about the commutative property of $5\frac{1}{2}$ groups of 6 compared with 6 groups of $5\frac{1}{2}$. I also wondered what would happen with the half when students tried to create $5\frac{1}{2}$ groups. How would they think about the half, and how would they express the half in their diagram?

When the noise settled to a calm hum, I called on another group.   85

Sonia: The answer will be the same no matter which way you do the problem. It doesn't matter because $6 \times 5\frac{1}{2}$ is the same as $5\frac{1}{2} \times 6$. Both of those are 33. I suppose you want a picture?

Sonia is one of my more proficient mathematics students. She tends to be quick to understand, quick to formulate an answer, and is usually not interested in drawing a diagram. However, I generally pretend I can accept nothing unless it can be proven with a diagram. So Sonia's group drew this on the board: 90

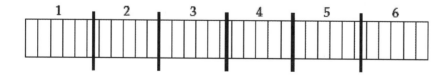

Victor: This picture shows $5\frac{1}{2}$ groups. There are 6 meters in each group except the last group. The last group only has 3 meters in it, because it is a half a group. 95

Teacher: What about an equation? [*Sonia wrote two equations on the board.*]

$$33 \div 5\frac{1}{2} = 6 \qquad 33 \div 6 = 5\frac{1}{2}$$

Daphne: We didn't do it that way, but I think it is the same thing. We kept adding.

$$5\frac{1}{2} + 5\frac{1}{2} + 5\frac{1}{2} + 5\frac{1}{2} + 5\frac{1}{2} + 5\frac{1}{2} = 33$$

Teacher: Is that the same, or is that different? 100

Daphne: It's a different way of doing the same thing.

Isaiah: You could subtract also. Just keep doing subtraction until you have zero. Oh! You would have to subtract six times!

$$33 - 5\frac{1}{2} - 5\frac{1}{2} - 5\frac{1}{2} - 5\frac{1}{2} - 5\frac{1}{2} - 5\frac{1}{2} = 0$$

The mathematics class was minutes from being over. Many of the students seemed to be 105
thinking about the meaning of the operations of division and multiplication. I knew that there
were many things I would like to have them discuss. Having a fraction in the problem did not
seem to pose much of an obstacle; I wondered if that was because the fraction was a half, and
many students had a special way of thinking about halves that did not always carry over to other
fractions. In the days to come, I hope to test this theory. 110

But of course, the students could not let me rest on my laurels too long. In the last two
minutes of class Philip confronted me with a new wrinkle.

Philip: When I do this the real way, I get a different answer: 6 remainder 3. [*He came to the board to show us.*] The 3 is half of 6. So the remainder is the half.

115

$$5\tfrac{1}{2} \overline{)\, 33 } \quad \begin{array}{r} 6r3 \\ \hline 33 \\ 30 \\ \hline 3 \end{array}$$

As everyone left, I thought to myself, "Half of what?" Now what do I do? Is this my lesson for
tomorrow? 117

8

Highlights of related research

by Lisa Yaffee

The cases in *Making Meaning for Operations* provide a glimpse of how students build an understanding of the four operations in classrooms where student thinking forms the basis of instruction. Although the story told by the cases is different in focus and in purpose from that conveyed by much of the formal educational research, the two accounts are complementary. 5 Both teachers and researchers are trying to define the issues students confront as they struggle to make sense of mathematics. Teachers write specifically about intriguing aspects of their students' thinking or learning, whereas researchers present ideas to support a theory or argument. Recently, however, the two approaches have moved closer together as researchers focus less on the ways individual children make sense of mathematics and more on interactions in classroom 10 environments and how they affect the learning process (Verschaffel, Greer, and De Corte 2007; Webb et al. 2014). Taken together, the cases and the research illuminate much of the rough conceptual terrain students must travel as they navigate among the features of the mathematical landscape.

Our goal here is to weave these two genres together, so that each of many viewpoints contributes to the others. Having worked with a set of classroom narratives, we now turn to what various researchers say about how students come to understand addition, subtraction, multiplication, and division.

Section 1

Modeling addition and subtraction

Children arrive at school with an intuitive understanding of mathematics. They are able to model and solve word problems without ever being taught how, using a variety of strategies.

Children derive informal mathematical knowledge from all aspects of their world. Setting the table, counting objects to compare quantities with someone else, pooling collections of items, creating and distributing equal shares of a coveted snack—these and other everyday experiences form the basis of the mathematical understanding children bring with them from home as they enter school. As Piaget (1965) and Dewey (1938) show, a young child's understanding of her environment is action based, and doing provides the substance for learning. The same is true when children encounter word problems for the first time. Without being shown anything formal about adding, subtracting, multiplying, or dividing, children act out the events described in the problems they see (Baroody and Standifer 1993; Carpenter, Fennema, and Franke 1996; Carpenter et al. 1999; Carpenter and Moser 1982; Carpenter, Moser, and Bebout 1988; Empson 2002a, 2002b; Empson et al. 2005; Hiebert and Behr 1988; Kamii and Warrington 1999; Mack 1993; Resnick and Singer 1993; Smith 2002; Verschaffel et al. 2007; Warrington 2002; Wing and Beal 2004).

Many of the actions children perform while solving addition and subtraction problems are derived from an understanding of counting and seem to develop along similar paths for most children. At first, students usually model all the quantities in a given problem by counting out objects to represent each distinct amount. Then they enact the problem situation by uniting or separating sets, finally counting the result. For example, when asked to solve the problem, "I have 6 rocks, and my friend gave me 8. How many do I have now?" children begin by directly modeling the action of the problem—putting out 6 objects to represent the first amount, 8 to represent the second, pushing the two sets together to form a single collection—then counting all the objects to get the total (Baroody and Standifer 1993; Carpenter et al. 1999; Fuson 1992, 2003; Gelman and Gallistel 1978; Steffe et al. 1983; Verschaffel et al. 2007).

What children do with the objects they use for modeling mathematics situations reflects their understanding of the structure of the situation. In the word problem described above, for example, the structure of addition is understood from physically joining quantities. Contexts that adults would recognize as simple subtraction might be interpreted in several ways by children—as separating amounts, as building on, as a comparison of parts to wholes, or as a comparison of unrelated quantities, depending on the context (Baroody and Standifer 1993; Carpenter et al. 1996; Carpenter et al. 1999; Fuson 1992, 2003; Mack 1993, Verschaffel et al. 2007).

In a problem such as, "Electra has 14 rocks and loses 6 of them. How many does she have   50
left?" many students assemble 14 items, remove 6, and count those remaining. Carpenter and
colleagues (1996; 1999) call this action *separating from*; the *Common Core State Standards
for Mathematics* (CCSSM) refers to such problems as *take-from*. In a problem such as, "My
friend has 6 rocks. After she picked up others, she had 14. How many more did she collect?"
students often put out 6 objects, add some more until the grand total of 14 is reached, and then   55
go back and count the number of things added. In this case the action performed is building on
or joining to. With a problem in which one person has 14 rocks, another has 6, and the question
is how many more the first person has, many students place 14 uniform objects in one row and 6
in a row underneath so everything is aligned, and then count the number of items in the row of
14 that stick out beyond the objects in the row of 6. The action performed here is *comparing*, in   60
which children use a matching strategy in order to identify the "extra." This is what Maya does
in case 5 when trying to figure out how many stickers one girl has, knowing that the total is 14
and the girl's friend has 6 of them (p. 13, lines 292–304).

    Although most conventionally schooled adults would probably call all the preceding
situations "subtraction problems" and would represent each of them with the same equation,   65
$14 - 6 = 8$, students often see these scenarios as qualitatively different from one another and
solve each problem using a different action, as noted. The different actions performed highlight
the distinct structures of various subtraction situations. Researchers classify these structures
as separate problem types (Baroody and Standifer 1993; Carpenter et al. 1996; Carpenter et al.
1999; Fuson 2003), which are each addressed in CCSSM. As we see in case 4, these are each   70
distinct problem types for many students. There, Zenobia has trouble recognizing the similarity
between a *missing part* problem (Max sees 3 blocks while his friend hides an unknown quantity
of the 7 blocks he started with) and a *missing change* problem (Max has 3 blocks and finds an
unknown amount to end up with 7 blocks). To Zenobia, one problem does "not really" resemble
the other in any way (p. 11, line 227).   75

    After children have modeled many situations in which they use objects to represent all
of the amounts in an addition or subtraction problem, they eventually need to show only one
of the quantities concretely. Initially students will represent the first quantity mentioned in a
problem, counting up or back from that amount and keeping track of the number of counts
made. Students later come to realize that it is easier to begin with the greater number and count   80
on by the lesser number. In the case of the rock problems, while finding out how many rocks my
friend and I have together if she has 6 and I have 8, someone might just count on from 8, putting
up one finger to represent each of the rocks in the other person's portion, until six fingers are
extended and six more numbers named. In the related subtraction scenario—my friend and I
have 14 rocks together; if I have 6, how many does my friend have?—a student might start with   85
14 and count back 6, because this requires fewer steps than starting with 6 and counting up 8
(Carpenter et al. 1996; Fuson 1992; Gelman and Gallistel 1978; Verschaffel et al. 2007).

    These counting up and counting back strategies mark a turning away from direct modeling
in that they require a more abstract concept of number than the earlier "show all quantities"

methods do. Children must understand the idea of *cardinality*—in other words, that a number   90
name or symbol stands for a constant amount—as well as a position in the counting sequence.
For instance, when counting rocks, 6 not only names the sixth number counted and stands for
the sixth stone reckoned, but it also represents the 5 additional stones previously included in
the count (Fuson 1992). Latasha's diagram of the valentine stickers in case 5 illustrates this
beautifully. The 6 stickers circled clearly include the previous 5, and the total of 14 stickers   95
also depicts the addends embedded in the sum at the same time that the two amounts exist
separately. In other words, as well as knowing that a number always contains the same quantity,
children must also understand that numbers, in this case the 6 stickers belonging to one girl and
the 8 belonging to the other, are parts of a larger whole as well as amounts in their own right.

100

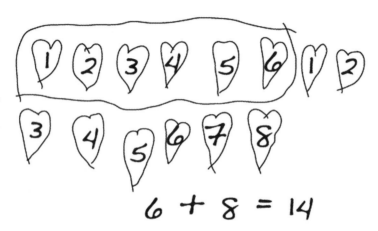

Fig. 8.1. Latasha's drawing of the valentine stickers

   Finally, children must be able to count from anywhere in a sequence and hold a double
count, keeping track of both the number of items they start with and the number that gets added
or separated (Fuson 1992). In case 2, Denisha knows that in order to determine how many girls
are in school when 2 out of 10 are absent, "You go down from 10 by 1, that's 9, and down 1   105
more, that's 8, so that's 2" (p. 6, lines 113–114). This kindergartner is able to count backward
correctly and monitor the number of counts made. She is still modeling the action in the
problem, but is doing it more abstractly than by putting out cubes to represent each child.

Section 2

Numerical reasoning begins

As students grow beyond the need to represent all of the amounts and actions in problems, they   110
no longer rely entirely upon counting to determine the results of joining or separating sets,
beginning instead to reason numerically about the quantities involved.

When children are able to pay attention to how all the amounts in a problem are related to one another, when they understand which numbers represent parts and which designate wholes, they are able to select solution strategies that don't mimic the specific action of the problem. Understanding how parts and wholes are related to one another in addition and subtraction problems also allows children to combine and separate quantities more flexibly. Students often use strategies based on facts they already know when they get to this stage. They take apart numbers and recombine them to form new quantities that they find easy to work with (Fuson 1992, 2003; Verschaffel et al. 2007; Fuson and Beckmann 2012). In case 5, for example, Cecile thinks about $6 + 8$ as if it were $7 + 7$, saying, "$7 + 7$ is easier for me to think about and that makes 14, so if I move 1 from one of the 7s to the other, I have $6 + 8$ and that is 14" (lines 000–000). Cecile no longer needs to represent the specific amounts in the problem, nor does she rely upon counting when she needs to add.

It is interesting that the growth from modeling all quantities and actions in a combining or separating problem to abstract reasoning with numbers is not a smooth or consistent transition for children. Some students appear to be at several levels simultaneously, able to count on when solving some problems but needing to model directly when making sense of a scenario that involves something harder, like separating or grouping, as shown by the kindergartners in case 8 when counting legs on bunnies and eggs in baskets. These children are mostly still modeling every quantity in a problem and counting to get the total. At the same time, some are also grouping amounts in an array format, constructing 3 rows of 4 cubes each to represent the number of legs on three bunnies, which is a conventional representation for multiplication. They haven't begun to actually multiply and are still modeling all of the amounts directly, counting by ones to find their answers, but they are starting to expand their concept of addition to include the idea of combining equal groups.

Section 3

Modeling multiplication and division

Although children come to an understanding of multiplication and division by modeling actions in a way similar to what they do for addition and subtraction, there are important and subtle differences.

One line of research suggests that children first encounter multiplication when having to combine several groups of the same size (Fischbein et al. 1985; Greer 1992; theory cited in Fuson 2003; and in Verschaffel et al. 2007). Students again begin by modeling directly all the quantities and actions in a given problem. When trying to find out how many cans are in 3 six-packs of soda, for example, a child may first count out 6 objects, next count out 6 more, and then create a third group of 6, finally counting all to get a result. As students move beyond the need to show every item in a group of objects, they use a more abstract counting strategy, just as they do for addition and subtraction. However, instead of representing one amount and counting up

115

120

125

130

135

140

145

or back from there, keeping track of the number of counts made, students might skip-count to or back from a given number while tallying the number of counts (Carpenter et al. 1996; Carpenter et al. 1999; Verschaffel et al. 2007).

In the addition or subtraction situation, students are counting individual objects, whereas in the multiplication or division scenario, they are counting both distinct objects and groups of objects. Thus, when adding the number of soda cans in 3 six-packs, a student may start at 6, count up 6 more to get 12 sodas with the second six-pack, and then count up 6 more to get a total of 18. In this case, the student is counting every soda can in each six-pack, **6**, 7, 8, 9, 10, 11, **12**, 13, 14, 15, 16, 17, **18**. When multiplying, the child might put up one finger and count, "6," another and say "12," and a third finger, saying "18." In this latter case of skip counting, each of the three fingers raised represents a group of 6.

Later, according to this line of research, students are able to keep in mind all of the amounts in a multiplication or division problem and can break up numbers to use them flexibly (Baek 1998; Carpenter et al. 1996; Fuson 2003; Verschaffel et al. 2007). Examples of students making sense of division at this level of abstraction, as well as a glimpse of how difficult it is to keep track of whether one is counting single objects or groups of objects when multiplying, are found in Janine's case 10. In this episode, three girls are trying to figure out how many packages containing 6 candy canes they would need so that each of 609 students could have one candy cane. Janine writes:

> Almost immediately the three decided that the problem had something to do with the 6 times table—and that they had to go pretty far up the table to get to where they wanted to be. They started "6, 12, 18, 24, 30," and soon realized that there had to be a faster way. (p. 38, lines 216–219)

> [One student knew that 6 × 9 was 54, so 6 × 90 would be 540.] From 540 they decided that they had to add up by 6s to get to 609. … Letitia, after some thought, said that 540 + 10 more would equal 600. One of the others said that 540 + 10 is equal to 550 and not 600. Letitia struggled to explain. … She knew that 10 was important, but couldn't hold onto the idea that it wasn't 10 but 10 *groups* of 6 she was thinking about. (p. 38, lines 226–232)

Letitia works this through, and her group decides that 90 packages and 10 more packages would provide 600 candy canes. Another package would bring them to 606, but they recognize that they would need still another package to supply 609 students with candy. Here, as in addition and subtraction, the children use relationships they already know in making sense of multiplication and division situations; and they also demonstrate that "skip counting isn't a pure strategy," but is often used with addition when the most familiar sequences (2s, 3s, 5s, 10s) aren't employed or when knowledge of a specific progression of multiples, in this case 6s, gives out (Empson, personal communication, May 20, 2008).

Just as students come to understand multiplication as a way of counting groups or as a form of repeated addition, they may understand division as a form of repeated subtraction. In case

11, for instance, Vanessa divides 8 into 24 by writing 24 − 8 = 16, 16 − 8 = 8, 8 − 8 = 0, and then writes 3 for the answer (p. 40, lines 263). We can see, then, that some of these processes are similar to the modeling and counting strategies children use to figure out what addition and subtraction are.

However, multiplication and division are different from addition and subtraction in ways that aren't instantly apparent. Addition and subtraction situations involve numbers that count or measure amounts directly. Each number represents a set of something, a simple quantity. Problems are solved by joining, separating, finding missing parts, or comparing sets, and the result is a third amount of the same kind as the other two: 3 donuts plus 4 donuts gives you 7 donuts (Carpenter et al. 1999; Dienes and Golding [1966] as cited by Harel and Confrey 1994; Fuson 2003; Hiebert and Behr 1988; Schwartz 1988). Multiplication, though, frequently involves two factors that represent different kinds of things; for instance, 3 bags each contain 4 donuts; how many donuts do I have? One factor is the number of sets, whereas the other is the number of items per set; both of these amounts must be tracked. The result is the quantity of donuts in all three bags, or in other words, the items contained in a set of sets (Greer 1992; Harel and Confrey 1994; Lamon 2006; Thompson and Saldanha 2003; Verschaffel et al. 2007).

To understand the idea of a set of sets, the child must be able to conceive of a collection as a unit (Harel and Confrey 1994; Lamon 2006; Thompson and Saldanha 2003). In case 8, we see at least two children working with this idea as they represent the number of eggs there would be in 3 baskets, each containing 3 eggs.

> Jenna used the interlocking cubes. First she made a unit of 3 cubes and brought them over to show me. I asked her what she had, and she said that she had one basket.
>
> "Where are the other baskets?" I asked.
>
> "I haven't made them yet," she said, heading back to the table. Soon she was back again, this time with two units of 3.
>
> "How many baskets do you have now?" (pp. 31–32, lines 56–61)

Jenna knows she has made two baskets and needs to make one more, which she goes off to do. Although she won't know how many eggs are in her 3 baskets until she counts them, she does realize that each group of 3 comprises a unit, namely 1 basket, and that each basket contains 3 items. Junior, however, is still building this idea. His model of the same problem consists of 3 orange cubes, 3 white cubes, and 3 yellow cubes. He knows he has 3 baskets, each containing 3 individual eggs, but when his teacher asks how many eggs he has in all, he says, "3." The teacher writes:

> Junior showed me how he counted: Each unit of 3 was "one" to him. I took one unit and broke it apart. He counted them, "1, 2, 3," and agreed that they represented 3 eggs. I put them back together with the other two units of 3 and asked him how many eggs were there. Again, he said, "3." I tried several ways to help him see that I wanted him

to count the individual cubes, but it didn't help. He was unable to see the difference or 225
sameness between cubes once they became a single unit of 3 (pp. 32, lines 80–85).

Whereas Jenna seems to understand the idea of a set of sets, Junior is still trying to figure
out how one unit can be comprised of multiple items and yet maintain its identity as both a single entity and as a collection of entities.

To summarize, then, one line of the research literature suggests that children first come 230
to understand multiplication as a way of counting groups, as just described, and then go on to
construct other meanings for it later, as we shall see. Much of this research tries to define types
of multiplication and division problems and examines student problem solving as it relates to
those types. We will look at these ideas more closely in the next section of this essay. However,
there is another group of researchers who find that students' ideas about multiplication and divi- 235
sion develop not out of counting but rather from experiences with sharing, in which equivalent
portions must be created. It is in dealing out these "equal shares" that students come to understand ratio, multiplication, and division as inextricably related concepts, inherent in the same
situations. They are doing this, in many cases, while still working on higher number counts and
while sorting out addition and subtraction concepts (Confrey 1995; Confrey and Harel 1994; 240
Empson 2001; Empson et al. 2005; Lamon 2006; Steffe 2002; Thompson and Saldanha 2003).

Consider, for example, the problem fourth-grade students were working on in case 22: "I
invited 8 people to my party (including me) and I only had 3 brownies. How much did each
person get if they had fair shares?" (p. 84, lines 12–13). Maribel still directly models the actions
of the problem, using pictures to create and allocate her portions: 245

For example … she drew 8 faces for the 8 people at the party and drew 3 brownies that
she cut into eighths. She then began distributing the pieces to the people. Each time she
distributed 8 pieces, she crossed out the brownie they came from. After she finished
distributing the pieces, she counted them up. "They each get 3/8," she wrote. (p. 84–85)

Maribel understands that this method results in equal groups, and she knows that the people 250
in the problem have equivalent shares without having to count the portions. Although she uses
counting to verify her solution, the actions she uses to solve the problem seem neither to be
rooted in counting nor, by extension, in repeated subtraction. Instead, they could derive from
an independent action which Confrey and her colleagues call *splitting*, the basic structures of
which are halving and doubling (Confrey 1988, 1995; Confrey and Harel 1994). 255

Although we don't see Maribel halving and doubling quantities in order to solve
multiplication and division problems, thereby working out an understanding of what those
operations mean, there are examples of students doing just that. In case 11 we see Cory working
on a problem in which someone is building bookshelves that require 4 boards each; the person
has 36 boards with which to work. Cory reads the problem and then comments to his teacher: 260

"I thought it was times." Then he reread the problem aloud. "See, that's why I
changed it to divided by. If it was 4 divided by, I would probably use 2 first so it
would be easier. First I would do 2 divided by 36, and that equals 28, and 2 divided

by 28 equals 14 … Because I knew divided by is half of whatever the
number is, like 2 divided by 100 is 50." (p. 41, lines 283–287)   265

To Cory, division means splitting a number in half, regardless of the structure of the problem. According to Confrey and a growing number of researchers, splitting numbers in half is a cognitive structure—an idea in terms of which other ideas are organized (Confrey 1995; Confrey and Harel 1994; Empson 2001; Empson et al. 2005; Lamon 2006; Steffe 2002; Thompson and Saldanha 2003). If we put aside the calculation error Cory's teacher helps him sort out moments later, we notice that   270 Cory sees multiplication and division as interchangeable and that his knowledge of both of them is developing simultaneously, which supports Confrey's contention that multiplication, division, and ratio co-evolve (Confrey, personal communication, February 3, 1997).

Section 4

Making meaning for multiplication and division

As students sort out the various contexts that can be modeled by multiplication and division, they   275 *continue to work on understanding the different types of units in these problems, deepening their knowledge of how the operations work and what they mean.*

As mentioned earlier, one branch of the research literature (the one which suggests that children first come to understand multiplication as a form of repeated addition and division as repeated subtraction) examines student problem solving as it relates to the type of problems being explored.   280 Three distinct types of multiplication situations have been categorized, each of which is related to a division situation as well. We discuss the three types of multiplication and their related division separately, the same way this research typically examines them.

We have already described one type of multiplication, in which the two factors represent different kinds of things—one, the number of sets, and the other, the number of items per set. Greer (1992)   285 and Kouba and Franklin (1993) call this type of multiplication *asymmetrical* because the multiplier and multiplicand play different roles and cannot be interchanged. As mentioned earlier, with the multiplication problem "3 bags, each containing 4 donuts; how many donuts do I have?" the two factors can't be used in place of one another. Three bags containing 4 donuts each $(4 + 4 + 4)$ is a different situation from 4 bags of 3 donuts each $(3 + 3 + 3 + 3)$, even though both involve 12 donuts.   290 If one person gets each bag, in the first case fewer people eat more donuts; in the second, more people eat fewer donuts. Because the two factors represent distinct types of units, the related division situation can be defined in two ways (Fischbein et al. 1985; Greer 1992; Kouba and Franklin 1993; Thompson and Saldanha 2003).

In one type of related division, known in the research literature as *partitive* and commonly called   295 *dealing*, an amount is split evenly between a certain number of groups. An example of this sort of "equal sharing" problem (Greer 's term, 1992) might be this: "You have 12 donuts to share equitably among 3 people. How many could each person have?" The result is the number of items in each group or portion. In the other kind of related division problem, known as *quotitive* or *measure* and

commonly called *grouping*, a quantity is split into shares of a certain size and the result is the number   300
of groups obtained: "You have 12 donuts. You want to make bags containing 3 donuts each. How
many bags can you make?" Though both problems can be solved using the same division equation,
$12 \div 3 = 4$, the solution to the first problem would be 4 donuts for each of 3 people, whereas the
answer to the second would be 4 bags with 3 donuts in each.

Students usually represent and solve these two types of problems differently. For a quotitive sit-   305
uation like the one in which 12 donuts are packed in bags of 3, the number of donuts in each group is
known and the number of groups is sought. To solve, students typically count out 12 objects and then
put them in piles of 3 until they run out (Carpenter et al. 1996; Kouba and Franklin 1993). Beyond
the direct modeling stage, students might skip-count (3, 6, 9, 12) to find out how many groups of 3
are in 12, or rely on their knowledge of multiplication facts (Carpenter et al. 1996; Fuson 2003). Here,   310
our classroom narratives contribute even greater detail to the research picture. In case 11, the students
come up with other solution methods: repeatedly subtracting 3 from 12 until there isn't anything left
to subtract from; adding 3 to itself to get 6 and then adding 6 to itself to get 12 (also documented in
Verschaffel et al. 2007); setting up a chart showing that 1 bag contains 3 donuts, 2 bags contain 6,
3 bags contain 9, and 4 bags would contain 12. Though the first method could be based on counting,   315
the last two might be considered splitting strategies, among possible interpretations.

When working on the partitive version of that same situation—"If 3 people are sharing 12 donuts,
how many donuts does each get?"— students use several direct modeling methods. The most common
is to select 12 items and then deal them one by one into 3 piles until they run out, counting the number
in each group to get the answer. Another approach is to count out 12 objects to represent donuts, guess   320
at a number that could go to each person, then deal out that many to see if any are left, and modify the
initial guess if needed. A third method is not to count out the total with which to begin, but simply to
create 3 groups of an arbitrary size, keeping track of how many objects are used up, until the total of
12 is reached (Kouba and Franklin, 1993; Verschaffel et al., 2007). There are, of course, more abstract
strategies as well—guessing an amount to skip-count by and seeing if it reaches 12, and then adjust-   325
ing the guess accordingly so that 3 counts are obtained or using known multiplication facts (Carpenter
et al. 1996; Verschaffel et al. 2007).

The second type of multiplication described through this line of research is called *symmetrical* by
Greer (1992) and by Kouba and Franklin (1993) because both factors play the same role, represent the
same type of unit, and can be interchanged. One of the most common instances of symmetrical mul-   330
tiplication is area; the length of a rectangle might be 4 feet and the width 3 feet until you rotate the
figure 90 degrees, when the length then becomes 3 feet and the width 4 feet. The same symmetry is
true of the array model. If you have a box of chocolates arranged 3 rows and 4 columns, you can turn
the box at a 90 degree angle and then have 4 rows and 3 columns. Another symmetrical form has
been called *cross-product* or *Cartesian-product multiplication*, an example of which is "If you own   335
4 shirts and 3 pairs of pants, how many different outfits can you put together?" (Greer 1992; Huinker
2002; Verschaffel et al. 2007).

Because the factors are interchangeable in these scenarios, there is only one type of related
division, that is, one in which a missing factor is determined. For example, if the area allotted for

the rectangular third-grade garden is 12 square feet, and we've already put 3 feet of fence along one side, how much fence will we need for a side perpendicular to the first? Although the factors in a symmetrical multiplication problem are the same kind of unit (items of clothing, linear feet of fence), the result of such multiplication is a unit different from that of the factors. *Items of clothing* times *items of clothing* become *outfits*, and *linear feet* times *linear feet* become *square feet* (Greer 1992; Kouba and Franklin 1993; Verschaffel et al. 2007).

The third type of multiplication involves comparison. For example, consider this problem: Today I walked twice as far as yesterday. Yesterday I walked 3 miles. How far did I walk today? Whereas additive comparisons involve adding to one quantity to result in the other, multiplicative comparisons involve multiplying one quantity to get the other. In this problem that compares the distance I walked over two days, the number of miles I walked yesterday is multiplied by 2 to find the number of miles I walked today: 2×3 miles $= 6$ miles.

In case 29, Selena gave her students this multiplicative comparison problem: A piece of elastic can be stretched to $5\frac{1}{2}$ times its original. When fully stretched, it is 33 meters long. What was the elastic's original length? In this problem, $5\frac{1}{2}$ is multiplied by the initial amount to get 33 meters, and the students were charged with finding the initial amount. Selena's students created different models to represent the problem, agreed the answer was 6 meters, and by the end of the class, they used the context to consider what is the same and what is different among the following equations:

$$5\frac{1}{2} \times 6 = 33 \text{ and } 6 \times 5\frac{1}{2} = 33$$

$$33 \div 5\frac{1}{2} = 6 \text{ and } 33 \div 6 = 5\frac{1}{2}$$

$$5\frac{1}{2} + 5\frac{1}{2} + 5\frac{1}{2} + 5\frac{1}{2} + 5\frac{1}{2} + 5\frac{1}{2} = 33$$

$$33 - 5\frac{1}{2} - 5\frac{1}{2} - 5\frac{1}{2} - 5\frac{1}{2} - 5\frac{1}{2} - 5\frac{1}{2} = 0$$

Section 5

Encountering fractions in sharing situations

As students model and solve problems that involve sharing quantities equally, they encounter a new type of number: fractions.

There is much evidence to suggest that children explore sharing problems and begin to build fraction concepts before they reach school (Cwikla 2014; Empson 1999, 2002a, 2002b; Hunting and Davis 1991; Hunting and Sharpley 1988; Mack 2002b; Piaget 1965; Sophian, Garyantes, and Chang 1997). Children encounter sharing situations early in their daily lives where they deal out a number of items and there is material remaining as well as where the number of sharers is greater than the amount to be shared (Charles and Nason 2002; Empson 1999, 2002a, 2002b; Flores and Klein 2005; Hunting and Davis 1991; Lamon 2006; Sophian et al. 1997).

An example of the first situation, in which children figure out what to do with the leftovers after dealing out items to share equally, is provided in *Building a System of Tens* (Schifter, Bastable, and

Russell 2016). The student April divides 143 jelly beans among 8 students, finding that each person would get 17 candies with 7 left over. The teacher writes the following description of how April   375
divided the remaining 7 jelly beans:

> Then she came up with a way to divide up the 7 extra jelly beans. She took 4 of them and divided each in half, so each of the 8 kids got $1/2$. Then she had 3 left over, so she took 2 of those and divided them into fourths, so each kid got an additional $1/4$. Then she divid-   380
> ed the last jelly bean into eighths, so each kid got another $1/8$. Now the question was how much was $1/2 + 1/4 + 1/8$? (p. 88, lines 285–292).

April resolves this by drawing a circle showing $1/2$, $1/4$, and $1/8$ inside of it. From this she can tell there is $1/8$ of the circle unaccounted for, so each child would finally end up with $17 7/8$ jelly beans. April, a fourth grader, obviously has much prior experience with dividing up quantities. She has already internalized the ideas that all the material needs to be used up and that everyone needs to   385
have the same-sized share, two concepts that children don't automatically bring to partitioning tasks, as we shall see in Lori's first-grade class later on in this essay (Hunting and Davis, 1991; Hunting and Sharpley, 1988).

Children also encounter fractions in whole number division contexts in which the number of people sharing exceeds the quantity of items to be shared. The students in cases 13 and 14 misread   390
the problem $39 \div 5$ as "5 divided by 39" and then try to make sense of this latter statement. At first they see the two equations as synonymous, a phenomenon well represented in the research literature, and then go on to claim, "You can't divide a number that's lower by one that's higher" (p. 49, lines 00–00), an idea forged by years of experience with whole number operations, and one that has also received research attention (Graeber and Baker 1992; Verschaffel et al. 2007). Several months later   395
when they revisit this problem at the next grade level, these students are able to visualize what 5 divided by 39 looks like by thinking about 5 candy bars shared among 39 people. Creating a context helps students see that "they would have to cut the 5 candy bars into little equal pieces" (p. 54, lines 147–148); and "each person would only get a really small piece, not anywhere like a whole candy bar" (p. 54, lines 170–171).   400

Although we see these students working to understand what fractions are and how they behave, much of the basic research about how children make sense of rational numbers has had a different focus. This work was done mostly in the 1980s and dealt predominantly with middle school and older children who spent many years in traditional classrooms, where memorizing the rules and procedures for solving computation problems formed the bulk of the mathematics program. The consequences   405
of such instruction are visible in the research, which examines patterns of errors made by students, reflecting common "misconceptions." The overwhelming impression is of children who have lost the ability, even the desire, to make sense of the mathematics they are doing, a picture that stands in sharp contrast to some of the current research conducted in classrooms like those in cases 13 and 14. So, with the caution that much of the early work about children and fractions focuses on what students   410
can't do and don't know, rather than on what ideas are in place and which ones are still under construction, we turn now to what the literature says is hard for children to understand about fractions.

Even though addition and subtraction of fractions still involve joining, separating, and comparing amounts, just as for whole numbers, Carpenter found in some of his earlier work that students don't see fractions as quantities, "but see them as four separate whole numbers to be combined in some fashion" (Carpenter [1976] as cited by Vinner, Hershkowitz, and Bruckheimer 1981). This finding was confirmed by the second and subsequent National Assessment of Educational Progress tests, in which students were asked to pick an estimate for $^{12}/_{13} + ^7/_8$ from the choices 1, 2, 19, and 21. Most students chose the latter two, presumably combining either numerators or denominators together. Following whole number addition procedures grown comfortable from years of rote usage, students lost the sense of $^{12}/_{13}$ and $^7/_8$ as quantities close to 1 (Behr, Wachsmuth, and Post 1985), or perhaps they had never developed that sense to begin with.

Stafylidou and Vosniadou (2004), in their study of 200 Greek students ages 10 to 16, also found children thinking about fractions as if they consist of separate whole numbers that bear no relation to one another just as much of the previous research did (Carpenter [1976] as cited by Vinner et al. 1981; Behr et al. 1984; Behr et al. 1985; Hartnett and Gelman 1998; Post and Cramer 2002). They point out that this lack of understanding emerges directly from a flawed generalization of the properties of counting numbers. Children assume that because you can determine the magnitude of a whole number compared to other whole numbers by its position in the counting sequence, the same will be true of fractions—but it isn't. With the counting of natural numbers, you always know where you are in the sequence because there is one unique number preceding and one following the number you consider. With rational numbers, there are an infinite number of quantities in between each count (Hartnett and Gelman 1998; Smith 2002; Sophian et al. 1997; Stafylidou and Vosniadou 2004). For example, $^5/_8$ is between $^1/_2$ and $^3/_4$; $^9/_{16}$ is between $^1/_2$ and $^5/_8$; $^{17}/_{32}$ is between $^1/_2$ and $^9/_{16}$; and so on. Where the counting numbers are discrete, fractions are dense. While there is a least natural number to which you can compare all other natural numbers, there is no least fraction (Stafylidou and Vosniadou 2004). In fact, the meaning of that smallest number expands when you consider the rational numbers. The unit no longer necessarily means a single entity. It can be a group of "several objects packaged as one" (Lamon 2006), and can be conceived in many different ways at once.

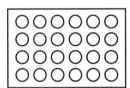

Fig. 8.2. A diagram of a case of soda

An example Lamon likes to use is a case of soda. The unit is the whole case. You can think of it as $^{24}/_{24}$ if you are picturing each bottle, which is $^1/_{24}$ of the whole. Or, you can think of the case as 4 six-packs and the whole becomes $^4/_4$. Each six-pack is $^1/_4$ of the whole, or $^6/_{24}$ if you are thinking about the same $^1/_4$ being made up of single bottles. If you visualize the bottles placed in the 6-by-4 arrangement of the case and then split that array down the middle horizontally, you can see that $^1/_2$

of the unit consists of 12 bottles, or two six-packs. Now the whole can be expressed as $^2/_2$, of which 12 bottles make up $^1/_2$, which can be thought of as $^{12}/_{24}$ in bottles, or $^2/_4$ if you are thinking about the half in terms of six-packs. If you choose to split the case vertically, looking at each column of 4 sodas in the box, the whole is now represented by $^6/_6$, of which those 4 drinks comprise $^1/_6$ or $^4/_{24}$ if you are defining the case as bottles. In all of these situations the unit is still the same—a case of soda—but suddenly it seems a lot more complex (Lamon 2002, 2006).

Thus we observe that when some of the ideas learned from years of counting are mapped onto all other sets of numbers, confusions can arise. As a consequence, some students have difficulty interpreting fractions as quantities. In fact, the entire idea of a quantity is challenged by fractions in that amounts are no longer "rendered when sets of things are counted. ... One cannot count things to generate a fraction" (Hartnett and Gelman 1998). However, sharing—an activity with which even young children have daily experience—does generate fractional amounts, as demonstrated in two examples we looked at earlier: the situation in which 143 jelly beans are shared by 8 people and that in cases 13 and 14 in which students determine how to share 5 brownies among 39 people. In those classrooms, the students have already had some experience with fractions. In case 15, we encounter first graders attempting to make the transition from whole number thinking to the kind of multiplicative reasoning required by fractions: many parts make up one set, or for every amount of this size, we have that amount. When asked how many brownies each of 4 friends would get if they were sharing 7, "many students came up with one of two different solutions. Either the students gave 1 brownie to each person and had 3 brownies left, or they gave 2 brownies to each person, giving 1 more brownie than was available" (p. 57, lines 231–233). Both of these responses to equal sharing problems are well documented in the research literature (Hunting and Davis 1991; Hunting and Sharpley 1988; Lamon 2006; Piaget, Inhelder, and Szeminska 1960). For those children who could conceive of shattering the unit whole, the sharing strategy they used was halving (p. 58. lines 249–256, 257–258) and repeated halving (pp. 58–59, lines 261–268), which confirms the masses of research literature that document the importance of one-half in children's developing conception of fraction quantities, equivalencies, and comparisons (Callingham and Watson 2004; Confrey 1995; Confrey and Empson 2002a, 2002b; Empson et al. 2005; Harel 1994; Moss and Case 2002; Piaget et al. 1960; Reys et al. 1999; Spinillo and Bryant 1991). The fact that most of these students gave each sharer "an equal number of pieces, but not necessarily an equal amount of brownies" (p. 59, lines 272–273), points to the dominance that whole number counting actions have over the children's conception of quantity.

It is not unusual for children to bring their informal knowledge of numbers to bear upon problem types they have never seen before. Their tendency with fractions is to split the units into fragments and to deal with each fragment as if it represents a whole number amount. Children can thus consider the number of pieces involved in a sharing task without ever having to understand that the amount of each piece is determined by the relationship between the parts and the whole (Kamii and Clark 1995; Lamon 1996, 2002, 2006; Mack 1993, 2002b). Even if the teacher had chosen to ask initially, "How much of the brownies would each friend get?" rather than "How many brownies?"—a question which implies a whole number response—the results would have been the same, for it is clear that these first graders have yet to develop an understanding of the unit as a set of sets which can be viewed as a simultaneous collection of any configuration of parts. They are just beginning to be able to split the whole while sharing, though several of them have yet to realize that portions must be equivalent, discrete, and that all the material must be used (Hunting and Davis 1991; Hunting and Sharpley 1988; Lamon 2006). Beyond that, they will have to be able to "reunitize" the whole—keeping in mind the size of the individual pieces as they relate to the size of the unit as well as the connection between the number of pieces in the whole and the size of each piece—while thinking relationally about how those shares might compare to ones created by other possible partitionings, since there is a variety of possibilities embedded in each item or set to be shared (Lamon 1996, 2002, 2006, 2007; Steffe, 2002; Tzur 1999). 490 495

Section 6

Understanding fractional amounts

When students begin to operate on fractions and other rational numbers, they need to perceive these new numbers as quantities in order to make sense of what fractions mean. 500

Being able to think about "how much" instead of "how many" while fracturing the whole to form composite units represents "an important conceptual leap … between additive and multiplicative reasoning" (Lamon 1996) because it implies the idea of comparison, which is what a fraction is. The value of a fraction is defined by comparing the two numbers that compose it. "It tells you how much you have relative to the unit," the meaning of which changes with each context (Lamon 2006). One-half is 2 out of 4 six-packs if using a part-to-whole interpretation of fractions; or 2 boys for every 4 girls if ratios are considered; or the amount someone gets if sharing one thing with another person or 5 things with a total of 10 people when the fraction is acting like a quotient; or the size of the photograph you get if you shrink the original 50 percent, where the fraction behaves as an operator; or the part of a foot of something measuring 6 inches in length when considering fractions in a measurement context (Kieren cited in Lamon 2001). If the unit in question comprises two items, half of this whole is one item. One-third of this same set is two-thirds of one item. Three-fourths of one item in a two item whole is three-eighths of the whole set. It is no wonder that a deep understanding of fraction concepts takes years to develop (Behr et al. 1984; Lamon 2006, 2007; Lappan and Even 2002; Reys et al. 1999). 505 510 515

The key to developing a robust understanding of fractions—what they are and how they behave—lies in understanding the idea of equivalence, which arises naturally in many problem contexts. Smith (2002) sees it when children are engaged in repeated halving. Steencken and Maher's students deal with equivalence as they are engaged in deciding which of two fractions is greater and by how much (2002). Lamon (1996, 2001, 2002, 2006) demonstrates that fraction equivalence is embedded in the idea of looking at the whole as different simultaneous configurations and recognizing how each is related to the others, as illustrated with the case of sodas in the previous section of this essay. Empson's students (2002b) encounter the idea of equivalence when they arrive 520 at several different answers to the same equal-sharing problem. The fourth graders in case 22 did the same while working on a two-part brownie-sharing problem: 8 children first share 3 brownies, and then share 2 more that are excavated from the bottom of the cookie jar. Some of the answers they obtained for this problem were $5/8$, $2/4 + 1/8$, $1/4 + 3/8$, and $1/2 + 1/8$. The teacher wonders if her students know that these expressions all stand for the same amount, suggesting that an understanding of equivalence is not automatic when working on sharing problems that yield the same amounts.

Empson, Smith, and others maintain that both partitioning procedures, such as repeated halving, and the ways children choose to represent what they are doing as they create equal shares, are how they first begin to make sense of equivalent fractions (Cramer and Henry 2002; Empson 2002a, 2002b; Moss and Case 2002; Smith 2002). Children create fourths by cutting halves in half, and then notice that $1/2$ is the same as $2/4$ and that $1/2 + 1/4 = 3/4$, based on their diagrams (Empson 1999; 2002a; Flores and Klein 2005; Smith 2002). The work of April, who drew a picture to figure out that $1/2 + 1/4 + 1/8 = 7/8$ (Schifter, Bastable, and Russell 2016) and case 19 in which Macario supported his argument that $1/4 = 2/8$ and Rabia proved that $2/6 = 1/3$ seem to confirm this.

It is clear then that equal-sharing problems can lead students to construct the idea of equivalent fractions but not without a significant amount of discussion. Empson says, "The way teachers talk with students about the fractional amounts they have created is central to the development of children's fraction concepts" (2002a). Other researchers (Behr et al. 1984; Cramer and Henry 2002; Kamii and Clark 1995; Lamon 2006, 2007; Steencken and Maher 2002) also attest to the number of experiences and conversations that are necessary before children are able to make sense of the idea that "two different fractions actually represented the same quantity" (Empson 2002b). This understanding requires knowing that when the units being partitioned are equivalent, the resulting portions are comparable—a key concept in ordering fractions (Steencken and Maher 2002). Specific procedures do not need to be committed to memory, and several researchers found that after a while, just by working with fraction equivalencies through equal-sharing problems, students were able to compare and order fractions of many different sizes, in spite of the difficulties usually encountered (Empson 1999, 2001, 2002a, 2002b; Empson et al. 2005; Flores and Klein 2005; Steencken and Maher 2002).

The trouble students have comparing and ordering fractions is known to all teachers and researchers, and some causes have already been implied in this essay. Children with years of experience in determining the value of a quantity by examining its position in the counting sequence are not going to be able to use that method to figure out the size of a fraction. Knowing that 5 comes after 2 and is therefore more than 2 does not help us compare $1/5$ and $1/2$. Similarly, $2/5$ cannot be deemed equivalent to $5/8$ simply because the difference between 2 and 5 is the same as the difference between 5 and 8. Nor can $3/4$ and $2/3$ be considered the same amount just because when you count back one from 4 you get 3 and when you count back one from 3 you get 2 (Post and Cramer 2002). Moreover, the language used to discuss fraction relationships often triggers counting-based conceptualizations of quantity that end up confusing children. When Post and Cramer asked students which fraction in a pair was more than the other, or which one was greater, students would often

525

530

535

540

545

550

555

560

respond, "Do you mean the size of the piece or the number of pieces?" (Post and Cramer 2002).

There are many studies about the strategies students use for determining which of a fraction pair is greater, and interestingly, most of them are illustrated by the cases in chapter 4 of this casebook. In case 17, Harry compares $\frac{1}{2}$ and $\frac{2}{3}$ by drawing a picture, which is the first approach children use to figure out how fractions relate to one another (Smith 2002; Empson 2002a, 2002b; Empson et al. 2005)—unless they are working with commercial manipulatives. Such materials offer the same type of physical modeling as drawing pictures, and they are easier for young children to deal with because the need for fine motor activity, such as cutting and drawing accurately, is obviated (Behr et al. 1984; Cramer and Henry 2002; Steencken and Maher 2002). However, these commercial materials often don't encourage the same kind of deep understanding and thinking that making one's own representations does (Empson 2002a, 2002b; Kamii and Clark 1995). Harry draws two rectangles of the same size, one divided in half with a horizontal line segment and the other in thirds. He shades in each of the amounts to be compared and can see that more is shaded in his picture of $\frac{2}{3}$, so he concludes that $\frac{2}{3} > \frac{1}{2}$.

Annie in case 17 also draws a picture in order to compare $\frac{1}{2}$ and $\frac{2}{3}$. She draws two circles of identical size, partitioning one in half and the other in thirds. She colors in $\frac{1}{2}$ of one and $\frac{1}{3}$ of the other. Because she knows that $\frac{1}{3}$ is less than $\frac{1}{2}$, she concludes that $\frac{2}{3} > \frac{1}{2}$. This method is documented in the research literature (Behr et al. 1984; Cramer and Henry 2002). In the same case, Gary uses a variation of Annie's method, forming mental images to compare $\frac{7}{8}$ and $\frac{3}{4}$, relying (like Annie) on a comparison of the amounts that aren't shaded but also looking at the distance of each fraction from 1. He pictures two equivalent squares, one split into eighths with 7 eighths shaded, the other into fourths with 3 fourths shaded. As he explains it, "You need $\frac{1}{8}$ more to make $\frac{7}{8}$ [into] a whole, and $\frac{1}{4}$ more to make $\frac{3}{4}$ [into] a whole. Since $\frac{1}{8}$ is smaller than $\frac{1}{4}$, then $\frac{7}{8}$ is larger."

Whereas Harry, Annie, and Gary are using pictures or a combination of pictures and numerical reasoning in case 17, Chuck is focusing on the numerical comparison between the numerator and the denominator in each fraction. He knows that the ratio between the numerator and the denominator in $\frac{1}{2}$ is 1:2 and that he needs to maintain the same 1:2 ratio between numerator and denominator in the second amount to show that the two fractions are equivalent. This means that if the denominator is 3, the numerator would have to be $1\frac{1}{2}$. Instead, he has a ratio of 2:3 between numerator and denominator in $\frac{2}{3}$, and because $2 > 1\frac{1}{2}$, he knows that $2 > 1$. Chuck is reasoning proportionally about these two amounts, and knows that the value of a fraction is determined by the relationship between the two amounts that compose it.

When asked to generalize some rules for comparing fractions, the fourth graders in case 17 are able to articulate several of the strategies that have been documented in the research literature. Ami's statement in that case, "when there's a 1 on top in both numbers, then the smaller denominator is bigger," implies an understanding of the inverse relationship between the number of pieces and their size (reported by Behr et al. 1984; Lamon 2006). There is proportional reasoning involved in knowing that the more pieces you have within the whole, the smaller they will be (Sophian et al. 1997), and Empson (1999) has seen this kind of understanding as early as first grade. Rea's method (case 17) also involves some proportional reasoning. When comparing $\frac{2}{8}$ to $\frac{3}{6}$ she knows that "3 is half of 6, but 2 isn't even close to 8," so by relating $2/8$ to $1/2$, a fraction she knows well, she is able to say that $3/6$ is larger. This strategy of comparing one of the fractions in a given pair to a different but common referent—like one whole, as Gary did above, or one-half, as Rea does here—is described by researchers, too (Behr et al. 1984; Cramer and Henry 2002; Lamon 2006; Reys et al. 1999; Smith 2002). 605

Bibiana, however, takes a totally different approach to determining whether $3/4$ is greater than $5/6$ in case 18. She does draw some pictures like many of the students in chapter 4, shading in one 6-by-6 grid to show $3/4$ and another to show $5/6$. But then, as one of her classmates puts it, Bibiana "translated 610 the fourths and the sixths into twelfths." She looks at the $1/4$ that isn't shaded in one picture, which consists of 9 squares within the 36-square whole; then looks at the $1/6$ that isn't shaded in the other, which consists of 6 squares, and sees they are both made from chunks of 3 squares. One chunk of 3 would be $1/12$ of the whole. Therefore $1/4$ of the whole would be made of 3 chunks with 3 squares in each, and $1/6$ would be made of 2 chunks of 3 squares. Because all of these portions can be defined in 615 terms of the same unit, namely chunks of 3—or twelfths—they are easy to compare.

To Lamon, this is one of the core ideas in developing a deep enough understanding of rational numbers to be able to use them in all their possible contexts. In addition to being able to visualize a fractional amount in several different ways simultaneously, according to which unit you choose to focus upon (like Bibiana does), it is also necessary to be able to compare numerators with 620 denominators within fractions and across them at the same time and to see whether or not all these amounts are changing in relation to one another (as Chuck is beginning to do). The fact that an "estimated … 90% of students entering high school do not reason well enough to learn high school mathematics and science with understanding," and about the same percentage of adults don't reason proportionally either suggests that this kind of multiplicative thinking does not "occur 625 spontaneously" and must be taught (Lamon 2006). The sort of teaching Lamon has in mind is exactly what is going on in the classrooms described in the cases. There is much research evidence which shows that building on students' informal knowledge of fractions by using problem situations drawn from daily experience will result in students who are able to understand what fractions are and how they behave and who can order fractions and operate upon them without ever being explicitly taught 630 a formal algorithm (Empson 1999, 2001, 2002a, 2002b; Empson et al. 2005; Flores and Klein 2005; Kamii and Warrrington 1999; Lamon 2001, 2006, 2007; Mack 2002b; Pesek and Kirschner 2002; Steencken and Maher 2002; Warrington 2002).

We see Bibiana invent common denominators in case 18 while responding to a problem posed by her teacher. Without any instruction in specific procedures, Bibiana has created the idea she needs to 635 answer the question "how much?"—an idea that is key to adding and subtracting fractional amounts. Jackson in case 22 is working on that same idea. While figuring out how much brownie a person gets if the amount is $1/4$ of one, $1/4$ of another, and $1/8$ of a third, Jackson begins to fall into a whole number rote memory trap, but then extricates himself as his understanding of the meaning of fractions kicks in. He explains: 640

> I was adding the $1 + 1 + 1$ [from the numerators] and it came to 3, but then I
> went to add the bottoms $[4 + 4 + 8]$ and it didn't make sense. There's nothing here

[in the problem] that's 16, and the numbers I was getting wouldn't match the brownies. ... I know the $1/4$ and $1/4$ make $1/2$, and then $1/8$. So ... each person had a share of $1/2$ and $1/8$ (p. 90, lines 132–137).

645

By focusing on the quantities the fractions signify, Jackson realizes that his original approach to the problem—attempting to fit addition and subtraction of fractions into his existing models for whole number computation—makes no sense, though it is a common occurrence among students to join and separate numerators with numerators and denominators with denominators (Behr et al.1985; Carpenter et al. 1996; Hartnett and Gelman 1998; Howard 1991; Stafylidou and Vosniadou 2004).

650

Jackson knows that $1/4 + 1/4 = 1/2$, but it is not clear whether or not he realizes that most of the time when we combine fractions, we add together numbers which are expressed as parts of the same-size implied whole. In other words, when thinking about $1/2 + 1/8$, we assume that both portions have come from brownies of equivalent size. Since the $1/2$ and the $1/8$ are defined relative to the same whole, they can therefore be understood as $4/8 + 1/8$. This idea of comprehending what the unit is—of knowing that when you add $1/2$ of something to $1/8$ of something, you are putting together quantities that are understood in relation to a third amount, the whole or unit—is difficult for children to grasp, but it is the same idea that the students in case 18 illustrate when they draw their comparative wholes as collections of 36 small squares.

655

Addition and subtraction of fractions can be further complicated for children by the fact that in some familiar, real-life situations that deal with ratios, adding numerators or denominators together is appropriate. For example, batting averages are computed by adding all the season's hits and dividing them by all the times at bat. If you get 5 hits in 8 times at bat during your first game, and 1 hit in 6 times at bat during your second game, then you are batting 6 for 14, or about .429. Field-goal percentages in hockey, soccer, and basketball are figured the same way—the total goals made per total attempted shots over the course of the season. In another scenario, if one pitcher of punch contains 2 cups of juice and 3 cups of ginger ale, and a second contains 4 cups of juice and 6 of cups ginger ale, then when you combine them, the new punch will have 6 cups of juice and 9 cups of ginger ale (Howard 1991; Lamon 2006).

660

665

670

Section 7

Revising ideas for operations with fractions

As the domain of number expands beyond whole numbers and into fractions, the ideas children have about operations, especially multiplication and division, frequently need revision.

When students move beyond addition and subtraction and into multiplication and division of fractions, their whole number interpretations of those operations, especially if they are based on counting structures, need revision (Siegler and Lortie-Forgues 2015). Repeated addition, for example, which makes sense when modeling multiplication of whole numbers or a whole number times a fractional amount, doesn't seem to work as well for multiplying two numbers that are less than a whole. For example, when children combine whole numbers or fractions more than one time, the

675

amounts they end up with are always greater than those they started with. Repeated addition of two fractions, though, is hard to comprehend. When considering $2/10 \times 1/2$ as repeated addition, what does it mean to add $1/2$ to itself $2/10$ of a time? Students need problem contexts that are meaningful as well as situations that help them see that multiplication no longer necessarily results in a number greater than either of the quantities operated upon (Hiebert and Behr 1988; Lamon 2006; Mack 2002a; Thompson and Saldanha 2003). 680

Several researchers suggest that an area model works well for illustrating multiplication of fractions, but that students first need to understand this model in connection with whole number multiplication (Graeber and Campbell 1993; Huinker 2002; Mack 2002a; Reys et al. 1999). Even with lots of previous whole number experience, students still have to work hard to make sense of how to compute the area of a rectangle with sides whose lengths include fractions. The students in case 26, for instance, have found the areas of countless rectangles with whole number dimensions, but when determining the area of a rectangle that has a width of $2^3/4$ and the length of $3^2/3$, it takes a while for them to realize that they "could indeed find the area of the entire region by taking all the things that [they] had counted," namely $2^3/4$ rows of $3^2/3$ units each, "and adding them together" (p. 102, lines 92–93). 685 690

When children encounter division of fractions, their whole number notions of that operation are also challenged. A number can now be divided by a greater number—contrary to what many students believe is possible, until they are shown contexts in which this would make sense, as, for example, when $1/2$ of a pizza is shared by 4 people (Graeber and Campbell 1993; Graeber and Tanenhaus 1993; Sinicrope, Mick, and Kolb 2002; Warrington 2002). Another conception about division that needs revising when dealing with fractions is the idea that division always "makes things smaller." In fact, the opposite is true if the divisor is less than one but greater than 0, as in the problem the teacher gave her sixth graders in case 28: 695 700

> You are giving a party. You have 6 pints of ice cream for the party. If you serve $3/4$
> of a pint of ice cream to each guest, how many guests can be served?

In this case, the answer is actually more than either of the numbers operated upon. 705

None of the case 28 students represent what's happening in the ice-cream problem with a division of fractions equation—an outcome that puzzles their teacher. The students base their choice of operation on what they perceive the mathematical structure of the situation to be rather than on the type or size of the numbers used, as the children in research studies often do. For example, one of the pupils took the 6 pints of ice cream and split them into 4 fourths each. That created "24 pieces, 3 pieces to a serving, 8 people can be served" (p. 109). The action performed by this student was grouping the 24 pieces by 3s, a division procedure, described by the equation $24 \div 3 = 8$. 710

By contrast, children in numerous studies of classrooms in which computation procedures were the focus of instruction chose operations for problem solving based on the size or type of the numbers involved instead of on the situation being modeled by the problem (Greer 1987, 1992; Bell, Fischbein, and Greer 1984; Bell, Swan, and Taylor1981; Fischbein et al. 1985). For instance, in one study when two problems with exactly the same mathematical structure but with different types of numbers were given, 12- and 13-year-olds picked multiplication to solve one and division to solve 715 the other (Ekenstam and Greger [1983] as cited by Greer 1992). The first problem, which they solved by multiplication, asked how much 5 kg of cheese cost if 1 kg costs 28 kroner. The second problem, which they solved by division, was essentially the same: how much would 0.923 kg of cheese cost if 1 kg costs 27.5 kroner? "It seems clear that the choice of division for the second problem is based on the realization that the answer will be less than 27.50, combined with the belief that multiplication always makes bigger, and division smaller" (Greer 1992, p. 288).

Conclusion

Although the vignette above and some of the other research described in this essay was conducted with children whose school mathematics experiences emphasized mastery of computation rather than making sense of number and operations, much of the research being done now focuses on classrooms like those described in the cases, where students are presented with problems to interpret and model in ways that make sense to them. In fact, the work of the educational researcher and that of the classroom teacher are moving closer together.

We read now of teachers engaged in "action research," studying how their students make sense of mathematics, often in collaboration with a college education program, or we read of researchers engaged in "teaching experiments," collaborating with public schools to see if the ideas for improved instruction emerging from the university are applicable and transferable to real classrooms (Adams and Sharp 2006; Empson 2001; Empson et al. 2005; Flores and Klein 2005; Gomez 2002; Lamon 2002; Steencken and Maher 2002). Teachers appear as guest lecturers in university courses, while education professors are teaching fifth-grade mathematics (Adams and Sharp 2006). The merging of effort between the research community and public school teachers was signaled at the turn of the millennium by the publication of books with titles like *Putting Research into Practice in the Elementary Grades* (Chambers 2002), in which researchers managed to maintain a separate identity and to offer the fruit of their independent labors to anyone interested. The efforts by the National Council of Teachers of Mathematics (NCTM), as in the series *Teachers Engaged in Research: Inquiry into Mathematics* Classrooms (Mewborn 2006), allow elementary and middle school teachers to publish their own studies with the help of mentoring professors, who use the information they glean from being in classrooms to help identify areas for further study. We also see educational researchers presenting experimental teaching protocols, problem sets, activities, and even fully developed curricula for teachers to use (Cramer and Henry 2002; Lamon 2006; Moss and Case 2002; Vanhille and Baroody 2002). These are often accompanied by brief classroom examples or narratives that sometimes read very much like the cases in this book, which are intended to help teachers anticipate the types of learning that can emerge with the use of these new materials or which attest to their efficacy (Cramer and Henry 2002; Lamon 2006).

There are countless similarities between what teachers describe happening in their classrooms and the descriptions researchers give of their own work. If we look at all of it together—the classroom cases and the formal or less formal educational research—the result is a richer and more nuanced picture than either discipline could produce alone. Together, they clearly depict the contexts being created to help students understand how real-life situations are represented by different types of numbers and operations. We are thus able to glimpse the complex process by which students internalize the mathematical structures of the problems they encounter. Though we may not fully understand this process, we can still recognize and support students as they move toward making meaning for the operations.   760

References

Adams, B., and J. Sharp. "The Impact of Classroom Research on Student and Teacher Learning: Division of Fractions." In *Teachers Engaged in Research: Inquiry into Mathematics Classrooms, Grades 3–5*, edited by C. W. Langrall, pp. 13–32. Greenwich, Conn.: Information Age Publishers, 2006.

Baek, J. "Children's Invented Algorithms for Multidigit Multiplication Problems." In *The Teaching and Learning of Algorithms in School Mathematics*, edited by L. J. Morrow and M. J. Kenney. Reston, Va.: National Council of Teachers of Mathematics (NCTM), 1998.

Baroody, A. J., and D. J. Standifer. "Addition and Subtraction in the Primary Grades." In *Research Ideas for the Classroom, Early Childhood*, edited by R. J. Jensen, pp. 72–102. New York: Macmillan, 1993.

Behr, M., I. Wachsmuth, and T. R. Post. "Construct a Sum: A Measure of Children's Understanding of Fraction Size." *Journal for Research in Mathematics Education* 16, no. 2 (March 1985): 120–131.

Behr, M., I. Wachsmuth, T. Post, and R Lesh. "Order and Equivalence of Rational Numbers: A Clinical Teaching Experiment." *Journal for Research in Mathematics Education* 15, no. 5 (Nov. 1984): 323–341.

Bell, A., E. Fischbein, and B. Greer. "Choice of Operation in Verbal Arithmetic Problems: The Effects of Number Size, Problem Structure, and Context." *Educational Studies in Mathematics* 15, no. 2 (May 1984): 129–147.

Bell, A., M. Swan, and G. Taylor. "Choice of Operations in Verbal Problems with Decimal Numbers." *Educational Studies in Mathematics* 12, no. 4 (Nov. 1981): 399–420.

Callingham, R., and J. Watson. "A Developmental Scale of Mental Computation with Part-Whole Numbers." *Mathematics Education Research Journal* 16, no. 2 (2004): 69–86.

Carpenter, T. P., E. Fennema, and M. Franke. "Cognitively Guided Instruction: A Knowledge Base for Reform in Primary Mathematics Instruction." *Elementary School Journal* 97, no. 1 (Sept. 1996): 3–20.

Carpenter, T. P., E. Fennema, M. L. Franke, L. Levi, and S. Empson. *Children's Mathematics: Cognitively Guided Instruction*. Portsmouth, N.H.: Heinemann, 1999.

Carpenter, T. P., and J. M. Moser. "The Development of Addition and Subtraction Problem-solving Skills." In *Addition and Subtraction: A Cognitive Perspective*, edited by T. P. Carpenter, J. M. Moser, and T. A. Romberg, pp. 9–24. Hillsdale, N.J.: Erlbaum, 1982.

Carpenter, T. P., J. M. Moser, and H. C. Bebout. "Representation of Addition and Subtraction Word Problems." *Journal for Research in Mathematics Education* 19, no. 4 (July 1988): 345–357.

Chambers, D. L., ed. *Putting Research into Practice in the Elementary Grades: Readings from Journals of the National Council of Teachers* of Mathematics. Reston, Va: NCTM, 2002.

Charles, K., and R. Nason. "Young Children's Partitioning Strategies." *Educational Studies in Mathematics* 43, (2002): 191–221.

Confrey, J. "Multiplication and Splitting: Their Role in Understanding Exponential Functions" in *Proceedings of the 10th Annual Meeting of the North American Chapter of the International Group for the Psychology of Mathematics Education*, (DeKalb, Ill., Nov. 1988): 250–259.

——— "Student Voice in Examining 'Splitting' as an Approach to Ratio, Proportions, and Fractions." In *Proceedings of the 19th International Conference for the Psychology of Mathematics Education*, vol. 1, edited by L. Meira and W. Carraher, pp. 3–29. Universidade Federal do Pernambuco, Recife, Brazil, July 1995.

Confrey, J., and G. Harel. "Introduction." In *The Development of Multiplicative Reasoning in the Learning of Mathematics*, edited by G. Harel and J. Confrey, pp. vii–xxviii. Albany, N.Y.: State University of New York Press, 1994.

Cramer, K., and A. Henry. "Using Manipulative Models to Build Number Sense for Addition of Fractions." In *Making Sense of Fractions, Ratios, and Proportions*, edited by B. Litwiller and G. Bright, pp. 41–48. Reston, Va: National Council of Teachers of Mathematics, 2002.

Cwikla, J. "Can Kindergartners Do Fractions?" *Teaching Children Mathematics* 20, no. 6 (2014): 354–364.

Dewey, J. *Education and Experience*. New York: Macmillan, 1938.

Empson, S. B. "Equal Sharing and Shared Meaning: The Development of Fraction Concepts in a First-grade Classroom." *Cognition and Instruction* 17 (1999), 283–343.

——— "Equal Sharing and the Roots of Fraction Equivalence." *Teaching Children Mathematics* 7 (2001), 421–425.

——— "Organizing Diversity in Early Fraction Thinking." In *Making Sense of Fractions, Ratios, and Proportions*, 2002 Yearbook of the National Council of Teachers of Mathematics (NCTM), edited by B. Litwiller and G. Bright, pp. 31–39. Reston, Va.: NCTM, 2002a.

——— "Using Sharing Situations to Help Children Learn Fractions." In *Putting Research into Practice in the Elementary Grades: Readings from Journals of the National Council of Teachers of Mathematics,* edited by D.L. Chambers, pp. 122–127. Reston, Va: NCTM, 2002b.

Empson, S. B., D. Junk, H. Dominguez, and E. Turner. "Fractions as the Coordination of Multiplicatively Related Quantities: A Cross-sectional Study of Children's Thinking." *Educational Studies in Mathematics* 63, (2005), 1–28.

Fischbein, E., M. Deri, M. S. Nello, and M. S. Marino. "The Role of Implicit Models in Solving Verbal Problems in Multiplication and Division." *Journal for Research in Mathematics Education* 16 (1985), 3–17.

Flores, A., and E. Klein. "From Students' Problem Solving Strategies to Connections in Fractions." *Teaching Children Mathematics* 11 (2005), 452–457.

Fuson, K. C. "Research on Whole Number Addition and Subtraction." In *Handbook of Research on Mathematics Teaching and Learning*, edited by D. A. Grouws, pp. 243–275. New York: Macmillan, 1992.

——— "Developing Mathematical Power in Whole Number Operations." In *A Research Companion to Principles and Standards for School Mathematics*, edited by J. W. Kilpatrick, G. Martin, and D. Schifter, pp. 68–91. Reston, Va: National Council of Teachers of Mathematics, 2003.

Fuson, K. C., and S. Beckmann. "Standard Algorithms in the Common Core State Standards." *National Council of Supervisors of Mathematics Journal of Mathematics Education Leadership* 14, no. 2 (2012): 3–19.

Gelman, R., and C. R. Gallistel. *The Child's Understanding of Number*. Cambridge, Mass.: Harvard University Press, 1978.

Gomez, C. "Multiplicative Reasoning: Developing Students' Shared Meanings." In *Making Sense of Fractions, Ratios, and Proportions*, 2002 Yearbook of the National Council of Teachers of Mathematics (NCTM), edited by B. Litwiller and G. Bright, pp. 213–223. Reston, Va.: NCTM, 2002.

Graeber, A. O., and K. M. Baker. "Little into Big is the Way It Always Is." Arithmetic Teacher 37 (1992): 18–21.

Graeber, A. O., and P. F. Campbell. "Misconceptions about Multiplication and Division." *Arithmetic Teacher* 40 (1993): 408–411.

Graeber, A. O., and E. Tanenhaus. "Multiplication and Division: From Whole Numbers to Rational Numbers." In *Research Ideas for the Classroom, Middle Grades Mathematics*, edited by D. T. Owens, pp. 99–136. New York: Macmillan, 1993.

Greer, B. "Nonconservation of Multiplication and Division Involving Decimals." *Journal for Research in Mathematics Education* 18 (1987): 37–45.

——— "Multiplication and Division as Models of Situations." In *Handbook of Research on Mathematics Teaching and Learning*, edited by D. A. Grouws, pp. 276–295. New York: Macmillan, 1992.

Harel, G., and J. Confrey, *The Development of Multiplicative Reasoning in the Learning of Mathematics.* Albany, N.Y.: State University of New York Press, 1994.

Hartnett, P., and R. Gelman. "Early Understandings of Numbers: Paths or Barriers to the Construction of New Understandings?" *Learning and Instruction 8* (1998): 341–374.

Hiebert, J. and M. Behr. "Introduction." In *Number Concepts and Operations in the Middle Grades*, edited by J. Hiebert and M. Behr, pp. 1–18. Hillsdale, N.J. and Reston, Va: Erlbaum and National Council of Teachers of Mathematics, 1988.

Howard, A. "Addition of Fractions—The Unrecognized Problem." *Mathematics Teacher* 84, no. 9 (1991): 710–713.

Huinker, D. "Examining Dimensions of Fraction Operation Sense." In *Making Sense of Fractions, Ratios and Proportions*, 2002 Yearbook of the National Council of Teachers of Mathematics (NCTM), edited by B. Litwiller and G. Bright, pp. 72–78. Reston, Va.: NCTM, 2002.

Hunting, R. P., and G. E. Davis. "Dimensions of Young Children's Conceptions of the Fraction." In *Early Fraction Learning*, edited by R. P. Hunting and G. E Davis, pp. 27–53. New York: Springer-Verlag, 1991.

Hunting, R. P., and C. F. Sharpley. "Preschoolers' Cognitions of Fractional Units." *British Journal of Educational Psychology* 58 (1988): 172–183.

Kamii, C., and F. Clark. "Equivalent Fractions: Their Difficulty and Educational Implications." *Journal of Mathematical Behavior* 14 (1995): 365–378.

Kamii, C., and M. A. Warrington. "Teaching Fractions: Fostering Children's Own Reasoning." In *Developing Mathematical Reasoning in Grades K–12*, 1999 Yearbook of the National Council of Teachers of Mathematics (NCTM), edited by L. V. Stiff and F. R. Curcio, pp. 82–92. Reston, Va.: NCTM, 1999.

Kouba, V. L., and K. Franklin. "Multiplication and Division: Sense Making and Meaning." In *Research Ideas for the Classroom, Early Childhood*, edited by R. J. Jensen, pp. 103–126. New York: Macmillan, 1993.

Lamon, S. "The Development of Unitizing: Its Role in Children's Partitioning Strategies." *Journal for Research in Mathematics Education* 27 (1996): 170–193.

——— "Presenting and Representing: From Fractions to Rational Numbers." In *The Roles of Representation in School Mathematics*, 2001 Yearbook of the National Council of Teachers of Mathematics (NCTM), edited by A. Cuoco and F. R. Curcio, pp. 146–164. Reston, Va: NCTM, 2001.

——— "Part-whole Comparisons with Unitizing." In *Making Sense of Fractions, Ratios and Proportions*, 2002 Yearbook of the National Council of Teachers of Mathematics (NCTM), edited by B. Litwiller and G. Bright, pp. 79–86. Reston, Va.: NCTM, 2002.

———— *Teaching Fractions and Ratios for Understanding: Essential Content Knowledge and Instructional Strategies for Teachers.* Mahwah, N.J.: Lawrence Erlbaum Associates, 2006.

———— "Rational Numbers and Proportional Reasoning, Toward a Theoretical Framework for Research." In *Second Handbook of Research on Mathematics Teaching and Learning*, edited by F. K. Lester, Jr., pp. 629–667. Charlotte, N.C.: Information Age Publishing, 2007.

Lappan, G., and R. Even. "Similarity in the Middle Grades." In *Putting Research into Practice in the Elementary Grades: Readings from Journals of the National Council of Teachers of Mathematics,* edited by D. L. Chambers, pp. 191–195. Reston, Va.: NCTM, 2002.

Mack, N. K. "Learning Rational Numbers with Understanding: The Case of Informal Knowledge." In *Rational Numbers: An Integration of Research*, edited by T. P. Carpenter, E. Fennema, and T. Romberg, pp. 85–105. Hillsdale, N.J.: Erlbaum, 1993.

———— "Building a Foundation for Understanding the Multiplication of Factions." In *Putting Research into Practice in the Elementary Grades: Readings from Journals of the National Council of Teachers of Mathematics*, edited by D. L. Chambers, pp. 145–149. Reston, Va.: NCTM, 2002a.

———— "Making Connections to Understand Fractions." In *Putting Research into Practice in the Elementary Grades: Readings from Journals of the National Council of Teachers of Mathematics*, edited by D. L. Chambers, pp. 137–140. Reston, Va.: NCTM, 2002b.

Mewborn, D. *Teachers Engaged in Research: Inquiry into Mathematics Classrooms.* Greenwich, Conn.: Information Age Publishers, 2006.

Moss, J., and R. Case. "Developing Children's Understanding of the Rational Numbers: A New Model and an Experimental Curriculum." In *Lessons Learned from Research*, edited by J. Sowder and B. Schappelle, pp. 143–150. Reston, Va: National Council of Teachers of Mathematics, 2002.

National Governors Association Center for Best Practices (NGA Center) and Council of Chief State School Officers (CCSSO). *Common Core State Standards for Mathematics. Common Core State Standards (College- and Career-Readiness Standards and K–12 Standards in English Language Arts and Math).* Washington, D.C.: NGA Center and CCSSO, 2010. http://www.corestandards.org.

Pesek, D., and D. Kirschner. "Interference of Instrumental Instruction in Subsequent Relational Learning." In *Lessons Learned from Research*, edited by J. Sowder and B. Schappelle, pp. 101–107. Reston, Va: National Council of Teachers of Mathematics, 2002.

Piaget, J. *The Child's Conception of the World.* Totowa, N.J.: Littlefield, Adams, 1965.

Piaget, J., B. Inhelder, and A. Szeminska. *The Child's Conception of Geometry.* London: Routledge and Kegan Paul, 1960.

Post, T., and K. Cramer. "Children's Strategies in Ordering Rational Numbers." In *Putting Research into Practice in the Elementary Grades: Readings from Journals of the National Council of Teachers of Mathematics*, edited by D. L. Chambers, pp. 141–144. Reston, Va.: NCTM, 2002.

Resnick, L. B., and J. A. Singer. "Protoquantitative Origins of Ratio Reasoning." In *Rational Numbers: An Integration of Research*, edited by T. Carpenter, E. Fennema, and T. Romberg, pp. 107–130. Hillsdale, N.J.: Erlbaum, 1993.

Reys, B., O-K. Kim, and T. Bay. "Establishing Fraction Benchmarks." *Mathematics Teaching in the Middle School* 8 (1999): 520–522.

Schifter, D., V. Bastable, and S.J. Russell. *Building a System of Tens Casebook.* Developing Mathematical Ideas Series. Reston, Va.: National Council of Teachers of Mathematics, 2016.

Schwartz, J. L. "Intensive Quantity and Referent Transforming Arithmetic Operations." In *Number Concepts and Operations in the Middle Grades*, edited by J. Hiebert and M. Behr, pp. 41–52. Hillsdale, N.J.: Erlbaum, 1988.

Siegler, R. S., and H. Lortie-Forgues. "Conceptual Knowledge of Fraction Arithmetic." *Journal of Educational Psychology* 107, no. 3 (Aug. 2015): 909–918.

Sinicrope, R., H. Mick, and J. R. Kolb. "Interpretations of Fraction Division." In *Making Sense of Fractions, Ratios, and Proportions*, 2002 Yearbook of the National Council of Teachers of Mathematics (NCTM), edited by B. Litwiller and G. Bright, pp.153–161. Reston, Va.: NCTM, 2002.

Smith, J., III, "The Development of Students' Knowledge of Fractions and Ratios." In *Making Sense of Fractions, Ratios, and Proportions*, 2002 Yearbook of the National Council of Teachers of Mathematics (NCTM), edited by B. Litwiller and G. Bright, pp. 3–17. Reston, Va.: NCTM, 2002.

Sophian, C., D. Garyantes, and D. Chang. "When Three is Less Than Two: Early Developments in Children's Understanding of Fractional Quantities." *Developmental Psychology* 33 (1997): 731–744.

Spinillo, A., and P. Bryant. "Children's Proportional Judgments: The Importance of 'Half.'" *Child Development* 62 (1991): 427–440.

Stafylidou, S. and S. Vosniadou. "The Development of Students' Understanding of the Numerical Value of Fractions." *Learning and Instruction* 14 (2004): 503–18.

Steencken, E. P., and C. A. Maher. "Young Children's Growing Understanding of Fraction Ideas." In *Making Sense of Fractions, Ratios, and Proportions*, 2002 Yearbook of the National Council of Teachers of Mathematics (NCTM), edited by B. Litwiller and G. Bright, pp. 49–99. Reston, Va.: NCTM, 2002.

Steffe, L. P. "A New Hypothesis Concerning Children's Fractional Knowledge." *Journal of Mathematical Behavior* 20 (2002): 267–307.

Steffe, L. P., E. von Glasersfeld, J. Richards, and P. Cobb. *Children's Counting Types: Philosophy, Theory, and Application*. New York: Praeger, 1983.

Thompson, P. W., and L. A. Saldanha. "Fractions and Multiplicative Reasoning." In *A Research Companion to Principles and Standards for School Mathematics*, edited by J. W. Kilpatrick, G. Martin, and D. Schifter, pp. 95–112. Reston, Va.: National Council of Teachers of Mathematics, 2003.

Tzur, R. "An Integrated Study of Children's Construction of Improper Fractions and the Teacher's Role in Promoting that Learning." *Journal for Research in Mathematics Education* 30 (1999): 390–416.

Vanhille, L. S., and A. J. Baroody. "Fraction Instruction that Fosters Multiplicative Reasoning." In *Making Sense of Fractions, Ratios, and Proportions*, 2002 Yearbook of the National Council of Teachers of Mathematics (NCTM), edited by B. Litwiller and G. Bright, pp. 224–246. Reston, Va.: NCTM, 2002.

Verschaffel, L., B. Greer, and E. De Corte. "Whole Number Concepts and Operations." In *Second Handbook of Research on Mathematics Teaching and Learning*, edited by F. K. Lester, Jr., pp. 557–628. Charlotte, N.C.: Information Age Publishing, 2007.

Vinner, S., R. Hershkowitz, and M. Bruckheimer. "Some Cognitive Factors as Causes of Mistakes in the Addition of Fractions." *Journal for Research in Mathematics Education* 12, no. 1 (1981): 70–76.

Warrington, M. A. "How Children Think About Division with Fractions." In *Putting Research into Practice in the Elementary Grades: Readings from Journals of the National Council of Teachers of Mathematics*, edited by D. L. Chambers, pp. 150–154. Reston, Va.: NCTM, 2002.

Webb, N., M. Franke, M. Ing, J. Wong, C. Fernandez, N. Shin, and A. Turrou. "Engaging with Others' Mathematical Ideas: Interrelationships among Student Participation, Teachers' Instructional Practices, and Learning." *International Journal of Educational Research* 63 (2014): 79–93.

Wing, R. E., and C. R. Beal, "Young Children's Judgments about the Relative Size of Shared Portions: The Role of Material Type." *Mathematical Thinking and Learning* 6 (2004): 1–14.